DAVID BUCKLEY

# God's Candidate for America

# God's Candidate for America

## for

## America

*Letting Your Light Shine in a Dark World*

by
John C. Hagee

First Printing, September 2000

ISBN # 1-56908-110-7

# Contents

## Chapter One
Let Your Light Shine .......................................................1

## Chapter Two
Family: God's Building Block for Society.................27

## Chapter Three
Abortion: The Line in the Sand .............................51

## Chapter Four
Euthanasia: The Desire to Escape Suffering............71

## Chapter Five
Gay Rights: A Moral Wrong ..................................97

## Chapter Six
Education: The Necessity of a Moral Foundation .............115

## Chapter Seven
Welfare: Christian Charity or Federal Handout?.................137

## Chapter Eight
Capital Punishment: Proportionate to the Crime .............153

## Chapter Nine
The Impact of Your Witness.................................167

## Chapter Ten
The Impact of Your Vote ....................................179

# Books by Pastor John C. Hagee

Being Happy in an Unhappy World

Should Christians Support Israel

The Power to Heal

The Beginning of the End

Take America Back

The Day of Deception

The Final Dawn Over Jerusalem

From Daniel to Doomsday

His Glory Revealed

God's Two Minute Warning

The Revelation of Truth

# 1 *Let Your Light Shine*

---

*This little light of mine,*

*I'm gonna let it shine . . .*


*Hide it under a bushel? No!*

*I'm gonna let it shine . . .*


*Let it shine, let it shine, let it shine.*


Several generations of Sunday School kids have grown up singing this restatement of a biblical principle originally set forth in the Gospel of Matthew: "Let your light so shine before men, that they may see your good works and glorify your Father in heaven" (5:16 NKJV). Like a lot of children's music, "This Little Light of Mine" is a simple song that presents a profound truth.

I really think we ought to starting singing this chorus in our adult church services. Without the hand motions, of course. That might ruffle the feathers of some of the saints sitting in the pews all dignified, sanctified, and petrified. On second thought, however, let's keep the hand motions. Let's stand to our feet, raise our index fingers in the air, and sing at the top of our lungs, "Hide it under a bushel? No! I'm gonna let it shine!" Maybe then the message would soak all the way from our heads down to our hearts.

You see, I'm not as concerned with ruffling feathers as I am with letting the light of the gospel shine with the power and force God intended. I look all around me and see that America is going to hell in a handbasket while the church has hidden the power of the gospel under a bushel basket. Instead of lighting a candle, we've been cursing the darkness. Instead of letting our light shine—instead of penetrating and vanquishing the darkness with the light of Jesus Christ—the church has become, to a large extent, a mere reflection of the decaying culture around us.

The gospel, however, is all about power—transforming power. "For I am not ashamed of the gospel of Christ," the apostle Paul wrote, "for it is the *power* of God to salvation" (Rom. 1:16). The early church understood God's power, but many Christians today have a false concept of it.

Do you ever wonder what it would be like to visit a New Testament church service? I imagine it would be a far cry from our stately sanctuaries with their crystal chandeliers, misty-mauve carpets, and uniformed ushers. The New Testament church was always in riot or revival—sometimes both at the same time. They were healing the sick, casting out demons, speaking in tongues, praising God . . . and being burned alive, thrown in the dungeon, and fed to the lions. There was no hiding the light of God under a bushel. The Christians of that era let their light shine so much, in fact, they were called the people who "turned the world upside down" (Acts 17:6).

Today, certain segments within the church focus primarily on the more dramatic manifestations of the power of God. These Christians go from church to church, from revival service to crusade meeting to prophecy seminar, searching for the latest spiritual thrills. The spectacular things these miracle-seekers chase after are not wrong; they are simply out of balance when they are made the focal point. I don't discount the supernatural power of God for a moment. As a pastor, I know for a fact that the miracle-working power of God has never ceased. Yes, we need to see more miracles in our churches, but most of all we need to let His supernatural power flow from the church into our world. We need to let our light shine.

The true power of the gospel encompasses a lot more than getting Holy Ghost goosebumps. Above all, it is the power to be witnesses. If you truly want to be an effective witness—if you want to let your light shine—then you must walk in the power of God's Spirit.

Jesus told His disciples—and, by extension, us—that they would do "greater works" than He had done (John 14:12). That was the purpose, Jesus said, for which God would send "the Helper, the Holy Spirit," after His own departure from the earth (John 14:26). That was also why He instructed His followers not to leave Jerusalem after His death and resurrection but to wait until the Holy Spirit baptized them (Acts 1:4–5).

Why did they need this Holy Spirit baptism? *To be witnesses.* "But you shall receive power when the Holy Spirit has come upon you; and you shall be witnesses to Me in Jerusalem, and in all Judea and Samaria, and to the end of the earth" (Acts 1:8).

The mighty power of God descended on the disciples on the Day of Pentecost much as the Holy Spirit had descended on Jesus when John baptized Him in the Jordan River. Jesus performed no miraculous works until this Spirit baptism had taken place. Later, He told His believers to wait for an anointing of power from on high before they started their ministry as well. He implied that they should not run out and attempt to fulfill the Great

Commission—going into all the world to make disciples (Matt. 28:19)—until they had received the same Spirit that had empowered Him. The disciples obeyed the command of Jesus, and ten days later God baptized them with Holy Ghost firepower. *Then* they proceeded to turn their world upside down.

The book of Acts is exactly that: the acts of the Apostles—after they were empowered by the Holy Spirit. History proves that the followers of Jesus did many mighty works—even "greater works," as He had indicated—following the Day of Pentecost. That same Pentecostal fire is still available today for any believer who is willing and yielded. The problem nowadays is that there don't seem to be large numbers of genuinely sold-out-to-Jesus believers. Modern churchgoers seem more interested in profits rather than stirring up the gift of prophecy. We're too busy running bake sales and bingo games to let our light shine.

Another significant problem is the widespread misconception that witnessing means preaching the gospel or, at the very least, handing out evangelistic tracts in a concerted effort. Of far more importance than these activities, however, is what might be called "lifestyle evangelism." That's a churchy sounding term for what the children's song says in these words: "This little light of mine, I'm gonna let it shine."

The concept of lifestyle evangelism is best illustrated by a quote from St. Francis of Assisi, who said, "Preach the gospel at all times; if necessary, use words."

Stop! Go back and read that last paragraph again.

Now, did you get that? Preaching does not require words. Your life is the best—or worst—sermon you will ever preach. *Who you are* is far more powerful a witness than *what you say.* God has called all of us to preach the gospel, although few Christians will ever stand in a pulpit to do so. We preach by the way we live before a watching world.

Sometimes the most effective witness for Christ is demonstrated in such simple acts as taking a loaf of home-baked bread to the family who just moved into the neighborhood. Sometimes witnessing to the power of the gospel means standing at a graveside and putting a comforting arm around a widow who faces a lonely, uncertain future. Sometimes it means buying a pair of shoes for a little boy walking barefoot on the hot pavement in the inner city.

That's preaching without words. When you reach out, not with a sermon but with a smile and support, then you earn the right to be heard. Then you can share the gospel message with a receptive hearer.

Paul wrote that believers are living "epistles . . . read by all men" (2 Cor. 3:2). In other words, your life is an epistle, or a letter from God, that will be read by everyone around you. How different our world would be if we truly understood that, if we lived our lives as an open book that continually testified to the radically transforming grace of God.

The dramatic Damascus Road conversion of Saul of Tarsus—the most zealous persecutor of Christians in his time—and his subsequent transformation by the working of the blood of Jesus Christ into Paul—the great evangelist and apostle who wrote thirteen of the twenty-seven books in our New Testament—represent one of the greatest proofs possible for the validity of Christianity. That's just how radical the changes were that God wrought in Paul.

We could transform our entire society if we would be willing, like Paul, to be radically transformed ourselves and then to let God transform others through the power of our witness.

Could your family, your friends, your neighbors find God by assessing the way you live? Would the light of your Christian walk point them to God? If Jesus Christ, the Light of the World, lives within you, and if the same Spirit that raised Christ from the dead empowers you—then your every action should point the way to God, and your every deed should give evidence of the truth of the gospel..

Are you a faithful representative of Christ? Are you a minister of God's love in your home, in your neighborhood, at your school, on your job? If not, you are part of the problem—and unless you change your witness, then your family members, your coworkers, your classmates, and your neighbors will spend an eternity in a demon's hell because you are a reproach to the name of Christ.

Consecration, taking up your cross, laying your life on the altar—none of these topics are as popular with Christians as teaching on prosperity, success, and current events. Yet it is the transformed life, the soul that has been reworked by the agency of the Holy Spirit, which compels the attention of those around us. If people look at you and cannot see God, then you do not have God—and God does not have you.

Until evangelical Christians become more like Mother Teresa and less like Ebenezer Scrooge, we are going to persuade very few that we have something spiritually they want. A "bah, humbug!" attitude toward a hurting world will not win the lost. A trite but true saying is that people don't care how much you know until they know how much you care.

*They'll Know We Are Christians . . .*

Oscar Wilde, the famous British playwright and cynic, once wrote, "Christianity is a great idea. Too bad no one has tried it." Bertrand Russell, the most famous atheist of the first part of the twentieth century, said that the reason he wasn't a Christian was that he knew too many Christians.

That's a tragic indictment of the followers of Jesus Christ. Tragic, but in so very many cases, all too true.

My own father, a man who cut his teeth on the back of a pew—a preacher whose entire culture was church people—once told me, "Son, whenever you do business with a Christian, always be sure you get a receipt." Why did my preacher daddy tell me that a receipt was necessary? Because of decades of experience with Christian hypocrites—he'd been burned by people who said one thing and did another. That's the kind of behavior that drew such scathing comments from critics like Wilde and Russell.

What *should* the world be saying about Christians? A folk song popularized by the Jesus Movement of the late '60s and early '70s said, "And they'll know we are Christians by our love, by our love. Yes, they'll know we are Christians by our love."[1] That's the thought expressed by Jesus in Scripture: "By this all will know that you are My disciples, if you have love for one another" (John 13:35).

Sad to say, these days one of the best ways to know if someone is a churchgoer is whether they are wearing their best clothes at a cafeteria on a Sunday afternoon.

Contrast that with what one ancient pagan wrote of the early followers of Jesus: "God! How they love one another." That same writer today might say, "Oh, God—how they strive to network and to sell to one another." The early Christians shook the world and changed history; modern Christians—all too many of them—have larger bankbooks than they have treasures laid up in heaven. Early Christians gave and shared and loved; modern materialistic Christians buy on time, are mortgaged to the hilt, and consider ostentatious consumption to be a virtue, not a vice.

Don't get me wrong. There is nothing unspiritual about making or having money—as long as you are a good steward of God's blessings to you. It's the attitude of your heart toward your wealth that God judges and the world watches. On the other hand, there is nothing noble or spiritual about being poor. You can drive a beat-up Volkswagen and wear a Timex watch and still have just as bad an attitude problem about money as the rich man who drives a Lexus and wears a Rolex. How tightly you hold on to what you have—whatever the amount may be—indicates your love for Christ and your fellow man.

A Christian's failure to "preach the gospel" with actions and deeds Monday through Saturday—in other words, by not living a life compatible with the beautiful words he spouts at church on Sunday—can cause people to fall away or be repelled by the gospel message. As a result, most people don't see the kingdom of God as exciting. Instead, they see Christianity as something to be endured—because all they've seen of God is *us*. Instead of life, we offer legalism; instead of liberty, we give them liturgy.

Do you claim to believe that there is a heaven and a hell and that unrepentant sinners will spend an eternity in a lake of fire after being judged by Almighty God? You do? Then have you ever left a church service with such a Holy Ghost concern gripping your heart for the eternal welfare of your lost family members and associates that you immediately go to them and contend for their eternal souls? Or do you just hurry out the doors of the sanctuary and head for a restaurant or go home to watch a ballgame? Is it that you don't believe there is a hell, or is it that you just don't care?

The word our English Bible translates as *repentance* comes from the Greek word *metanoeo*, which means literally "a changing of the mind" or "a changing of the way you think." We have many churchgoers today who need a changing of their minds.

A genuine convert from sinful living to Christ will demonstrate works and fruit consistent with repentance. Unfortunately, the church today is too accepting of people who are nothing more than role-players; and they turn honest, inquiring people off with their evident sinful inconsistencies. Jesus called such religious play-acting hypocrisy.

*Take Off Your Mask*

> *Woe to you, scribes and Pharisees, hypocrites! For you cleanse the outside of the cup and dish, but inside they are full of extortion and self-indulgence . . . Woe to you, scribes and Pharisees, hypocrites! For you are like whitewashed tombs which indeed appear beautiful outwardly, but inside are full of dead men's bones and all uncleanness. Even so you also outwardly appear righteous to men, but inside you are full of hypocrisy and lawlessness.*
>
> Matthew 23:25, 27–28

When Jesus called the Jewish leaders of His day "mask-wearers" or "pretenders"—that's what the Greek word *hupokritase* literally means—He was likely speaking from the vicinity of one of the hillside amphitheaters around the Sea of Galilee. If Jesus were walking the streets of America today, it would be like preaching to Christian leaders just outside the gates of a major Hollywood film studio or perhaps a great Broadway theater.

Whatever the location, the people listening to Jesus knew He was talking about actors and role-playing. And what dumbfounded them was that He used theater terminology in reference to their religious leaders, who were very offended by the lewd Greek and Roman dramas regularly presented in the numerous amphitheaters as well as indoor theaters. "You religious leaders are no better than the lowlife actors in the plays you criticize. You both wear masks"—that's the gist of what Jesus was preaching.

He came down hard against showy, superficial religious leaders, accusing them of religious pretense. Jesus said these people were trying to present a public image completely different from who and what they really were. They demanded things of their followers they weren't willing to do themselves. They made a great show of their religion, placed great stock in appearing spiritual. They were outwardly beautiful but inwardly rotten, having the stench of death. *Hypocrites.*

Such pretenders are repugnant to God—and their practices have turned many people away from Him. One thing street evangelists and altar workers can tell you is that many people have rejected or turned from "The Way"—which is how early believers referred to the Christian walk—because of things so-called Christians had done, or not done, to them.

Our Lord took a stand against the Jewish religious leaders having one set of rules and conduct for synagogue and another entirely different set of rules for home or for business dealings. Today, Jesus would rail against the Sunday version of Christianity that allows a person to act one way at church and another way at home or on the job. Psychologists call that a cognitive disconnect. That's just a fancy way of saying that a person's actions and thinking don't match up. If God is truly in control of your life, it should be evident twenty-four hours a day.

Let's look at a few examples of how this hypocritical mask-wearing can keep Christians from letting their light shine. In later chapters we'll look at some of these issues in more depth.

You say you believe in the equality of man, that you believe racial discrimination is wrong. Do you attend a church where people of all races and ethnic origins are welcome, or do you belong to a homogeneous church where everyone looks and acts the same? Do you have any friends or close associates outside your own ethnic group, or could an outside observer be justified in assuming you are prejudiced because of *appearances?* I know Christians who would never drink a glass of ginger ale or a cola in a restaurant bar because they don't want people to even suspect they might be drinking alcohol—yet those same people think nothing of ignoring people of color and of being completely indifferent to racial injustices still occurring every day in America.

My Bible says nothing about a white church, or a black church, or a brown church. It simply talks about the blood-bought church of Jesus Christ. So why is 11:00 A.M. on Sunday one of the most segregated hours in our nation? It's a blight on Christianity.

You say you are against abortion. What have you done personally, and what does your church do, to assist young girls in trouble? Do you provide counseling? Do you offer food, medical, and financial support and help with the ultimate decision to place the child in a loving adoptive home? Or do you merely cavil against teen pregnancies as you eat Sunday luncheon with your other church friends? People who work for Planned Parenthood aren't necessarily demons from hell, you know. Although I believe they have been deceived and are unwittingly on the side of hell in this debate, they are caring people trying to assist women in trouble. Are you as quick to help your local crisis pregnancy center as you are to criticize Planned Parenthood?

Those of you with sons and grandsons and nephews, are you doing your part to educate your boys about morality? Somebody is getting those young girls pregnant. Are you making them take responsibility for the babies they help make because of their immorality? What are you doing to make a real-world difference in the lives of the hurting people facing difficult choices in their own personal abortion debate?

Homosexuality is a sin: the Bible is crystal clear about that. But why do we act as though a homosexual or lesbian is any worse a sinner than a tax cheat, a thief, a murderer, or a hypocrite? In many ways, AIDS patients are the lepers of our day. Many of them are dying painful, impoverished, terribly isolated deaths because Christians by and large have not figured out that compassion toward the sinner does not equate to condoning his sin.

I'll be honest with you. Homosexual behavior is a sin I've never been troubled with, and it's a sin I don't understand. But I know that Jesus doesn't love homosexuals any less than anybody else. And if Jesus loved them and died for them, then as Christians we must reach out to them. There's no place for hatred or name-calling. I simply cannot picture Jesus walking a picket line carrying a placard reading, "Queers and Faggots Will Burn in Hell."

Welfare reform has been a major political hot button ever since Lyndon Johnson's Great Society legislation back in the middle 1960s. Since then over five trillion dollars in government aid has been paid out to the financially challenged in our country. Yet the percentage of those with incomes under the poverty level has not changed since liberal government activists started taking money from the pocketbooks of those who were working and giving it to those who refused employment. The welfare program in this country has shattered the family structure of the lower-income families who accepted government assistance, driving males out of the household, and virtually guaranteeing generational dependence on the dole.

I'm not bashful about speaking out against what I see as a failed policy that created this moral and economic morass. At the same time, I believe the church cannot close its eyes to the truly needy in our midst. We are not obligated to finance the lazy lifestyles of those who can work but won't. "If a man will not work, he shall not eat" is the rule Paul laid down for the New Testament churches (2 Thess. 3:10 NIV).

Yet James wrote that looking after "orphans and widows in their distress" is "religion that God our Father accepts as pure and faultless" (1:27 NIV). A few verses later he wrote, "Suppose a brother or sister is without clothes and daily food. If one of you says to him, 'Go, I wish you well; keep warm and well fed,' but does nothing about his physical needs, what good is it?" (2:15–16 NIV).

When we debate issues like welfare reform, abortion, or homosexual rights, we must remember that poor people, pregnant women, and homosexuals are not our enemies. Our battles are not with flesh and blood. We are fighting a spiritual war—a war for the hearts of men, women, and children across this land.

We must be living the gospel in the smallest of deeds if we want to influence our nation for good in the greatest of issues. There must be a theme of goodness and consistency that runs through each of our lives if we want to set ourselves up as representatives of Christ in the political and social arenas.

### What Would Jesus Do?

Bracelets and T-shirts with the letters *WWJD* on them have been extremely popular among Christian youth for the past several years. The letters stand for "What Would Jesus Do?" Now, there's a question each of us should ask ourselves as we go about our business affairs and daily interactions with everyone we encounter. But, amazingly, this concept of "What Would Jesus Do?" has not really caught on among adult Christians. It's as though *WWJD* is a good idea for the kids, but it doesn't apply to us more mature types—an unwarranted conclusion, for sure, since Jesus is clearly presented as our example in Scripture.

In light of the previous discussion, let's think about "What Would Jesus Do?" in relation to our Lord's admonition against being hypocrites.

Let's say you are a businessperson. How would Jesus run your business? Would He make the same decisions you make every day? How would He treat your customers? Your employees? Are you so busy being profitable on Monday that you forget you were a Christian on Sunday? Do you strive to maintain the highest possible standards of morality, integrity, and honesty? Or do you take advantage of your customers' dependence and complete trust? Do you practice the Golden Rule or does mere gold rule?

Suppose you are a housewife. Are you like the woman described in

Proverbs 31, who builds her home into a haven of love, a refuge from the cares of the world? Or do you have an atmosphere of immorality and verbal filth in your home because of the soap operas, talk shows, and cable movies you view each day?

Parents, do you wonder if your child will serve God? Children are not stupid. All a child has to do is sit around and watch, to take inventory of how things are done—or not done—around your home. Let me tell you, a parent who gives their children "hell" every Sunday morning in order to get them to church on time has a severe theological dysfunction. Imagine: sarcasm, criticism, verbal abuse, strife, and ill temper—all because they can't wait to get to the house of peace. Maybe the parent is a volunteer worker, a musician, an usher, or an elder. If so, you can bet he or she will be nothing but smiles and cordiality upon arrival at the church house. This same church leader will then wonder why their children rebel and their teens have little inclination for the house of God.

Now, I ask you. Is that letting your light shine?

Do you have a Christian bumper sticker on your car? I hope you do—if you are a courteous driver. When you voluntarily advertise your association with Christ—whether through religious medallions, bumper stickers, T-shirts, and the like—you have a responsibility to be a 24/7 witness of God's goodness. And if you aren't a good witness—for example, honking and waving and gesturing at someone who cuts you off in traffic—people will notice. Road rage is never acceptable conduct for a person who is supposed to be modeling light to the world.

Let me make it clear, when you take it upon yourself to identify with Christ but then live inconsistently with the role you are acting out, you give those who are looking for reasons not to believe a chance to shake their heads and smile and make fun of the gospel. You're giving the body of Christ a black eye.

### *Can You Relate to the Debate?*

As we've discussed, letting your light shine means living a life consistent with biblical principles. It also means getting involved in the world around you—and especially getting involved with . . . hold your breath . . . sinners. That's right. As much as we enjoy fellowship with like-minded believers, we cannot stay in our Christian enclaves and win the lost. We need to form relationships with unbelievers.

Let's see. "What Would Jesus Do" in this situation? You know the answer to that. He was criticized for fellowshipping with tax collectors and sinners. Did it stop Him? Of course not. Jesus said He came "to seek and to save what which was lost" (Luke 19:10 NKJV), and He did not hesitate to share with sinners in social settings, not just preach to them.

Unfortunately, many Christians have taken the admonition to be "in the world, but not of it" to mean total separation from the world. These just-say-no Christians have an ostrich mentality—they keep their heads stuck in the sand, hoping that the problems in our government and our society will just go away. At best they're willing to pray about issues, but not willing to roll up their sleeves and tackle them.

I'm not undermining the power of prayer; I'm being faithful to Bible principles. God is not going to miraculously zap all our problems away when we pray. He called us to be salt and light, and He expects us to get busy and change the things that are in our power to change.

We must engage our culture in the political debate. To do so successfully, we must be able to express ideas in terms the secular world can understand. No more Christianese, please! It's like speaking a foreign language when we try to employ our private jargon in the secular arena.

One of the great New Testament examples of a Christian engaging the culture is found in Acts 17:16–34. In this passage we find Paul in Athens, reasoning in the synagogue with the Jews, and debating the Greek philosophers in the marketplace. Eventually, he was invited to a meeting of religious leaders on Mars Hill. Paul knew what these philosophers and religious leaders believed, and he quoted their own poets to turn their attention to God. He noted an inscription on one of their monuments—TO THE UNKNOWN GOD—and used that as his starting point.

People haven't changed in two thousand years. In Paul's day, "all the Athenians . . . spent their time doing nothing but talking about and listening to the latest ideas" (Acts 17:21 NIV). And to think, they didn't even have the help of CNN's 24-hour news coverage or commentary by Dan Rather, Peter Jennings, or Tom Brokaw.

Today, people not only feast on satellite news broadcasts, they revel in the endless babble of TV and radio talk shows. Like the Athenians, we avidly discuss all the latest ideas and philosophies. The Mars Hill debate is still going on—are you able to represent your Christian beliefs confidently when your fellow citizens parrot the latest thing they've heard on Oprah or Jenny Jones? You might decry the daytime talk shows, but they are addressing issues that people are thinking about.

Letting your light shine means bringing God's word to bear on every situation and every issue. Many people involved in the current debate think the Bible doesn't speak to modern culture. Skeptics and critics like to point out, for example, that the Bible does not mention the word homosexuality. While it is true that particular word does not appear in the pages of the Bible, the concept certainly does—and in unmistakable terms: "You shall not lie with a male as with a woman. It is an abomination" (Lev. 18:22 NKJV). Similarly, the Bible does not speak about abortion. But biblical principles certainly apply to the present abortion debate in America.

The purpose of this book is to get you thinking about what is happening in your world politically and socially, because letting your light shine means taking your faith into the secular arena where decisions are being made on issues that affect you and your family. By no means is this book an exhaustive look at the issues, but it's a good starting point.

Another thing we'll look at is how to energize a grassroots groundswell of God-believing citizens who can lay siege to the school board, to city hall, to the state house, all the way to Congress, the White House, and the Supreme Court. We'll talk about how to get involved in the election process and how to influence public opinion. If you follow the gameplan set forth, you will be equipped to begin the process of making a difference in the governmental, educational, and judicial power structures of your world.

As you journey through the world of political activism, however, you must always remember that who you are, and how you live your daily life, will mean far more to those in society than anything you will ever say or any vote you will ever cast. To claim the high moral ground in any political fight, you must be a moral person living a moral life, fighting in a moral cause. You have to "walk the walk," not just "talk the talk."

Back in 1992 I began preaching a series of sermons called *Take America Back.* I said then that the solution to our problems is for the church to come together in unity . . . to stop fighting each other and start fighting the forces of Satan . . . to speak out for righteousness . . . to be bold as a lion . . . and to take America back one heart at a time, one home at a time, one city at a time.

I haven't changed my thinking one iota since then. More than ever I believe the church of Jesus Christ must let our light shine upon America so that through the power of our witness we can reach this last generation for Jesus Christ.

Where, then, shall we start? Let's begin with the family, God's building block for the church and for society.

# 2 *Family: God's Building Block for Society*

By God's design, the family is the fundamental building block for society, and it has been that way since the Creation. The first chapter of Genesis says that "God created man in His own image ... male and female He created them" (1:27). In the second chapter, a more detailed account is presented. There we learn that God formed the first human being out of the dust of the ground, and he called the man Adam. Yet this man was not the culmination of God's creation. A second human being—like Adam and yet, oh, so different—was needed to complete the basic unit of human society: a husband and wife.

We are not told how much longer after the creation of Adam this additional creative act took place, but it was long enough for Adam to get bored with naming the animals and long enough for Adam to want fellowship beyond his evening walks with God (Gen. 2:19). The Creator and His creature were not equals; therefore it is not surprising that Adam needed a companion more like himself. "It is not good that man should be alone," God said. "I will make him a helper comparable to him" (Gen. 2:18).

Possibly it was the fact that God could come and go and Adam had to remain in the garden that caused Adam to be lonely. He was less than happy, yet Adam did not know what he needed. Our God, however, who knows what we need before we can even think to ask for it, knew exactly what Adam needed.

God caused a deep sleep to come over Adam, and while he was under the divine anesthetic, God removed a rib from his side (Gen. 2:21). Sometimes God has to take something from us we don't really need in order to give us something that, in His divine providence, is even better for us. On this occasion, God took a rib from Adam and fashioned a woman out of it. And when He presented the woman to the man, Adam was content at last. Finally, all those hormones God had given Adam had a place to go, and Adam was supremely happy with this final creative act. God told the happy couple to "be fruitful and multiply" (Gen. 1:28).

Once God had a functioning family unit in place—once Adam had a companion—God considered that His creation was complete. Family is the building block God has ordained for society, for procreation, for financial security, and even for evangelism. That is why, ever since, Satan has been working full-time to do everything he can to erode, to dilute, and to destroy the family unit. Anything that will demean the sanctity of the marriage bond or derogate the uniqueness of family ties, Satan has attempted.

If there is no family, then there is no home. With no positive home life, there is no security and no haven from the strife and pressures of daily living. With no rest, in an environment of constant stress and recrimination, children grow up unsettled and adults start to have health problems. People become self-centered and selfish from having to constantly strive and grasp to keep their own personal misery levels as low as possible. Satan wants every day of your existence to be a walk through the valley of the shadow of death—and one way he tries to accomplish that is through stripping you of the benefits, love, and approval of family. Because Satan wants to blast the family unit apart like a Fourth of July fireworks explosion, he will stop at no device, hesitate at no evil to accomplish his desire. If he can get a businessman to find his pleasure in work, if he can get a woman to find her companionship and understanding outside of the home, if he can get the children to feel a stronger identification with school or sports than with family, then Satan has succeeded in his work.

We see Satan's attack against the family in a variety of spiritual and societal ills. Abortion, abuse, adultery, covetousness, disunity, divorce, enmity, financial troubles, homosexuality, lesbianism, love of money, murder, strife—all are works of the flesh, tools Satan uses to attack this fundamental, God-ordained, building block of human relations.


*The eternal value of extended family*

In the last few decades we have heard a lot about the *nuclear family*—a family unit comprised of a father, a mother, and one or more children. While many conservatives decry the breakdown of the nuclear family and point out the problems stemming from children growing up in broken homes—and I'm one of the critics—some commentators are now pointing out that the larger problem is the breakdown of the extended family. God designed the so-called nuclear family to function as part of a larger network, an extended family of parents, children, grandparents, aunts, uncles, cousins, etc. Let's look at the value of maintaining this extended family as a vital network of relationships.

First, of course, is the fundamental relationship of husband and wife. The importance of the contribution of the right woman to a man's success in life has been demonstrated through the millennia. After all, that's why God created Eve—as a companion suitable for Adam. If Adam could have made it on his own, there would have been no need for Eve. Any student of biography and history can tell you that a man who has achieved great accomplishments has either had the extreme approval of a mother who doted on him or the unqualified support of a wife who loves him. Even secular success guru Napoleon Hill, author of the number one personal goal-achievement book of all time, *Think and Grow Rich*, wrote that one of the major causes of failure in business and personal life is due to the wrong selection of a mate in marriage. This is not rocket science we're talking here—this is basic common sense about human relations.

There is a reason that positive contributions made by men without the stabilizing influence of a good woman are very hard to find. Solomon, known as the wisest man of biblical times, agreed with God's assessment that it was not good for man to be alone. Solomon wrote:

There was a man all alone;

he had neither son nor brother.

There was no end to his toil

yet his eyes were not content with his wealth.

"For whom am I toiling," he asked,

"and why am I depriving myself of enjoyment?"

Eccl. 4:8 NIV

Just like Adam, the man Solomon described needed a companion, not just to help him through life but to help him enjoy the fruits of his labor.

Two are better than one,

because they have a good return for the work:

If one falls down,

his friend can help him up.

But pity the man who falls

and has no one to help him up!

Also, if two lie down together, they will keep warm

But how can one keep warm alone?

Eccl. 8:9–11 NIV

The husband and wife, that first union necessary to build a family, produce offspring, according to God's design; then the parents and children together form the basic building block of society. Solomon said that children are a gift from God or a "reward"—the "heritage of the Lord"—and that a man's children are to him like a quiver full of arrows in the hands of a warrior (Ps. 127:3).

Parents have an obligation to raise their children in a godly home according to godly principles, and children have an obligation to honor their parents and care for them in old age, just as the parents cared for the children when they were helpless and dependent. Most of the problems our society faces today stem from the failure of the family unit to operate as God intended it.

If parents down through the ages had been the parents God intended them to be, the Great Commission would already be fulfilled. Ephesians 6:4 instructs parents to bring their children up "in the training and admonition of the Lord." If all parents lived the reality of the gospel before the watching eyes of their children, we would have revival unparalleled since the Holy Ghost outpouring in the Upper Room in Jerusalem. There's a good reason teenagers don't wear bracelets that spell out "What Would Dad Do?" or "What Would Mom Say?" Teens can point to too many inconsistencies they've observed in the adults around them.

Beyond parents and children, aunts, uncles, cousins, and especially grandparents are important—extended family is vital. One reason I believe God gave grandparents is to keep mothers and their teenaged daughters from killing each other! Young children benefit from a grandparent's love and attention. Many's the child who has been won to the Lord at a grandparent's knee. Teens and young adults can benefit from a grandparent's love and intercession when a parent messes up. Adults benefit from an older relative's wisdom, life experience, and understanding.

An example of the value of the uncle-nephew relationship is the relationship between Abraham and his nephew Lot. For whatever reason, Abraham ended up being the one who nurtured and groomed and taught his nephew how to be a man. Another example of extended family in action would be how Simeon and Elizabeth took Elizabeth's pregnant-out-of-wedlock cousin Mary in for a while before her marriage to Joseph.

As these examples demonstrate, there is tremendous value in maintaining a close relationship among extended family members. For one thing, overlapping adult nurture, counsel, and oversight will probably mean fewer teenage pregnancies and less rebellion. With all those adults around, it's harder for kids to get away with stuff when they do decide to act up. But most important of all, children within a close-knit extended family will grow up with a knowledge of who they are and a genuine sense of significance. Children need a sense of belonging—they need to feel they matter to the people they love. Research indicates that young people raised in this kind of environment tend to avoid negative conduct as children and make fewer wrong choices as teens. Further, as adults, they seem not to be as plagued by feelings of inadequacy and undefined identity crises—especially in mid-life—as are those who never developed a true sense of personal identity.

### God's command to preserve the family unit

No wonder, then, that God's word stresses the importance of keeping the family unit together. Let's look at some of His commandments that deal with preserving the sanctity of the family, specifically the marriage union and the parent-child relationship.

The Seventh Commandment prohibits sexual relations outside the marriage union: "You shall not commit adultery" (Ex. 20:12). The Bible says that the male-female bond is so intimate, so charged with electricity, that when a man and woman come together in marriage, they become like one flesh (Gen. 2:24; Matt. 19:5–6). Many erroneously believe that "one flesh" is a reference to the act of sexual love. It's not—although sexual love is a vital part of a happy marriage relationship. What the term really means, to use modern imagery, is that in a marriage the man and woman are and welded or melded together. That is the original sense of "one flesh." The violation of this incredible bond through the sin of adultery is so severe in God's eyes that he originally prescribed stoning to death—capital punishment—for the guilty parties in an adulterous relationship (Lev. 20:10).

The Tenth Commandment is against coveting: "You shall not covet your neighbor's house; you shall not covet your neighbor's wife ... nor anything that is your neighbor's" (Ex. 20:17). Note that it specifically forbids coveting your neighbor's wife—or your neighbor's husband, by extension. If you are coveting your neighbor's spouse, you are not living a consecrated life and you need to repent of the sinful thoughts you've entertained and the lustful desires you've allowed to take root in your heart. As a young boy I was always told that you can no more prevent wrong thoughts and temptations from entering your mind than you can prevent birds from flying over your head—but you can prevent the birds from building a nest in your hair. The Bible says sin starts after you give wrong thoughts a chance to incubate, germinate, and proliferate—sin is the fruit of the crop of bad seed you allowed to take root in your life. Don't cast a lustful eye at somebody else's husband or wife. Center your fantasy life on your spouse, and focus your energies on building a life and achieving your dreams with your marriage partner.

The Fifth Commandment instructs children to honor their fathers and mothers (Ex. 20:12), and it is the only commandment with the promise of long life. It is restated in the New Testament in these words: "'Honor your father and mother,' which is the first commandment with promise: 'that it may be well with you and you may live long on the earth'" (Eph. 6:2–3). Unfortunately, many a frustrated parent has used this commandment like a lash to beat an angry child. Yes, children are to honor and respect and obey their parents. It's not negotiable. But to counterbalance possible parental abuses of this commandment, the apostle Paul added words to the effect that parents were also to treat their children with similar respect. Immediately after he said that children must honor their parents, he said: "And you, fathers, do not provoke your children to wrath" (Eph. 6:4). The New International Version translates this verse: "Fathers, do not exasperate your children."

Granted, that's not an easy task. Parents and children are often prone to exasperate each other. But, as adults, the greater responsibility is on parents to make sure they instruct and train and correct their children without provoking them to anger. Why? Aside from "doing unto others as you would have them to do unto you" it's because no human is as totally dependent for life and emotional health as a young child. This is an absolute principle from God, that parents are to be kind and fair and mindful of their children's mental and emotional needs as they raise them in the admonition of the Lord. As a pastor I have counseled with many adults who were wounded emotionally by their parents and who, decades later, are still trying to deal with unkind words and parental acts of omission and commission that scarred them.

One man, a leader in his church, was constantly critical of his teenaged son's grades. It didn't matter that the boy might have gotten five A's and one B+ on his report card. That was not a cause for celebration. That one B+, which was in a subject the boy hated and the father had never taken the time to tutor him in, was proof in the father's eyes that the boy was not trying hard enough. Years later, when his mother was going through an envelope of old family keepsakes and photos, the boy saw his father's old high school report cards. The grades were all C's and D's. This Christian young man—an honor student who had won national recognition for his scholarship and had been a contestant in the state debate championships—became angry and hurt and *exasperated* when he realized his father had maintained a double standard. The father had never once told his son, "You're doing a great job—I'm proud of you." He never said, "I'm glad you're doing better than I did in school." The dad never said, "If B+ is the best you can do, that's all I expect." Instead, this dad said, "Your best isn't good enough." Is it any wonder that son suddenly felt his father had been dishonest and unfair? Situations like these make for anger, resentment, mistrust, and bitterness between soon-to-be-adult teens and their parents.

Such situations also damage the parent-child relationship and the biblical commandments to honor and provide for each other. Part of "honor your father and mother" is the obligation of children to care for their parents in their old age. I do not believe that means seeing to it they get into a good nursing home and then abandoning them there. Jesus implicitly referred to this biblical mandate to care for elderly parents. Railing against hypocrites—the mask-wearers—He said that just as it is wrong to go and worship when know unresolved hard feelings exist between two believers, it was wrong for grown children to give money to the work of the Lord when their parents were in financial need. "For Moses said, 'Honor your father and mother.' … But you say that if a man says to his father or mother: 'Whatever help you might otherwise have received from me is Corban' (that is, a gift devoted to God), then you no longer let him do anything for his father or mother. Thus you nullify the word of God by your traditions that you have handed down" (Mk. 7:10–12 NIV).

Why would Jesus say to support your parents instead of the work of the Lord? Because, aside from the sanctity of the family, in those days there were strict inheritance practices. A father would bring his son into his business and then literally give it to him, passing on the family wealth from generation to generation. Our equivalent these days would be to send your son or daughter to college and then to make a place for him or her in your business. It's not hard to understand why such ingratitude and indifference to someone who had made your wealth possible would anger God. Imagine you had given your children everything you had been able to accumulate in order to set them up in business, and then they let you starve while they spent their inheritance to build a new wing onto the church. That would be *dishonoring* your father and mother while claiming to honor God.

Children, remember your parents—and parents, with all that is in you, raise your children in the love of the Lord and strive to make it easy for them to love, honor, and revere you. Not only is it the right thing to do, it will pay you tremendous dividends in your advanced years as your physical strengths start to decline and your finances start to be stretched.

*Dissolution of the family structure*

In modern times we are reaping the consequences of unraveling the close-knit family. We live in a very mobile, very materialistic society, and the tendency today is to sacrifice the extended family unit on the altar of mammon. Sadly, extended families are often exploded when one member receives an offer of making a few thousand dollars more a year—if they would only move a few hundred miles away. When families separate, for the best and seemingly noblest of reasons, families can suffer. In a sense, the family is like a bunch of bananas—once you get separated from the bunch, you are liable to get peeled.

There has been a tremendous increase in the number of financially capable families—families with comfortable incomes and sufficiently large homes—who warehouse their infirm parents in nursing homes. That never happened when I was a boy; we weren't rich enough to cast our old folks off. None of us were rich enough—and it would not have occurred to us if we were—to warehouse our aged and infirm loved ones in a "constant care" facility. I use the word *warehouse* on purpose. You rent a storage unit to get rid of things you have no room for in your house—and you stick grandma in a nursing home to free up bedrooms and make more "free time" for the younger, more active family members.

Cultural practice in the old Eskimo Inuit culture allowed people to set their elderly parents out on ice floes and let the icy Arctic currents carry their old folks out to sea to either drown or else die of exposure. But that was okay, to their pagan way of thinking, because their aged relatives were too old and infirm to pull their own weight around the igloo. That's what too many families have done to our seasoned citizens in America today. The dissolution of the family unit can be every bit as severe and complete at the steps of a nursing home as it can be in the stirrups at an abortion parlor. And a private "suite" at a nursing home can be every bit as cold, lonely, and hostile as a windswept ice floe bobbing in the Arctic Ocean.

God's plan is for aged parents and grandparents to continue as vital parts of their family, ideally under the same roof with their loving family members. Granted, there are times when a nursing home or institutional setting may be medically necessary, times when a parent or grandparent requires care that simply cannot be given at home. But for a large percentage of the elderly in nursing homes, that is not the case. In addition, many options, such as hospice care, are available to help keep even the very sickest patients at home with their families.

Children are constantly observing and learning, and they will learn from watching their parents' example of love, respect, nurture, and esteem—or lack of it—to older friends and loved ones. If you have warehoused grandma and forgotten her except on major holidays, you are modeling for your children your own future neglect—you are demonstrating to your children that it is okay to wash your hands of weak, disabled, and economically dependant persons. You might as well tattoo Dr. Kevorkian's phone number on your forehead for them to use when you get old.

While career moves and assisted living facilities have scattered the extended family, a skyrocketing divorce rate has broken up the nucleus of the family: mom, dad, and the kids. Couple the divorce rate with the tremendous increase in out of wedlock births, and the statistics are grim: by age eighteen, six out of every ten children in the U.S. are living apart from one of their biological parents.[1]

The social and economic consequences of the breakdown of families have been devastating. "Children of broken families drop out of school more frequently, become sexually active at younger ages, have higher rates of crime and drug abuse, and earn lower incomes as adults."[2] Parents who divorce raise children with higher expectations of divorce. "The risk of divorce in the first five years of marriage is 70 percent higher for daughters of divorced parents than it is for daughters from intact marriages."[3]

Approximately half of all marriages end in divorce today—and the problem is no better inside the church than it is outside. There is nothing about being a Christian that should cause any person to have to divorce. There is no such thing as "incompatibility" for two people claiming to be Christians—how can the Jesus in the husband be incompatible with the Jesus in the wife? If there is incompatibility in a Christian home, then you have at least one person in that home who is not living a Christ-centered, consecrated life. Even when a Christian is married to an unbeliever, divorce should not be the norm. The apostle Paul said that any follower of Christ who was married to an unbeliever should strive to stay married and not seek a divorce unless his or her spouse abandons the relationship (1 Cor. 7:12–13).

Jesus said not to seek a divorce unless sexual sin was a factor (Matt. 5:32). I would add a further corollary, however: if your spouse is physically abusive to the point of endangering your or your children's health, or if he or she is guilty of incest, or if your partner completely violates the sanctity of the home due to criminal conduct or extreme substance abuse, then you should prayerfully consider what God would have you to do. God hates divorce, and the Bible instructs us to endeavor to live at peace with all men (Heb. 12:14)—but getting beaten to death for the glory of some denomination's entrenched teaching is not what God requires.

Another outcome of the divorce epidemic is that it deprives the children of the attention of not just one but both parents: one (usually the dad) is no longer living in the home, and the other (usually the mom) is forced to spend more time in the workforce. One study showed that on average 80 percent of all divorced dads do not ever see their kids within twenty-four months after the divorce. Sadly, for whatever reason, the end result is almost as though the children had divorced their father. While it's true that most of those fathers abandon their relationship with their children, other divorced dads complain that their ex-wives won't let them see their children. Let me say this, if you have children from a previous marriage, for the sake of the children as well as your eternal soul, do the right thing. Don't manipulate or play games with your ex-spouse using your children as pawns, and don't isolate your children from your ex-spouse.

Not all absentee dads are physically absent, however. Most of them are emotionally absent—dads who spend every night under the same roof as their children yet are too busy to spend any time with them. Several surveys have been done over the past decades, and in each case the numbers are virtually the same: the average dad spends less than a minute a day face-to-face with his children.

Psychologists say there are two ways to know if a person really believes in something they claim as a priority value in their life, whether it's church, sports, children, a spouse, or a hobby. You gauge whether a person has taken "ownership" of that value or priority by how much money and how much time they invest in it. If you say church is important to you but you never give and you never attend—guess what? Church is not important to you. If you say your children are important to you but you never have time to play catch, or to attend their ball games or choir recitals, or even to talk to them—guess what? Your children aren't important to you.

One of the biggest hits of the early 1970s' music scene was Harry Chapin's ballad "The Cat's in the Cradle." The song was about a father who had no time for his son, who was supposedly his pride and joy, when the boy was young. The son grew up saying, "I'm gonna be like you, dad. You know I'm gonna be like you." The dad was always so busy making money—doing the urgent things—that he had no time to do the important things like spend time nurturing and developing his boy into a man. Well, the boy grew into a man anyhow—but because he had grown up alone and independent of his father, when Dad retired and wanted his son to come by with the grandbabies, the son just couldn't find the time. The father finally realizes, "My boy was just like me."

People love to say that "quality" time is the key for happy, healthy, well-adjusted children. Others say that it's the quantity of time that's important. Kids will tell you that it's *all* the time. Young kids are like dry sponges in a drought—they can't soak up enough of your love, they can't receive enough positive feedback, and you can't spend too much time with them. And you're smart to spend the time—because there will come a time when, if you haven't been making large deposits in their emotional savings account, you will start writing checks you don't have emotional equity on deposit to cover.

You invest in your businesses—invest in your family, invest in your kids. Men, if you have time to golf or to watch a football game, you have time to spend with your kids. Ladies, if you have time to spend hours shopping at the mall or playing tennis or watching TV, you have time to make sure your family eats at least one meal sitting down, together, as a family each and every day.

Some kids are rebellious for a reason. Some of them are so starved for attention that they go out and color their hair purple or blue or chartreuse. They have so many facial piercings—in the ears, cheeks, eyebrows, nose, lips, and tongue—they look like they drove a motorcycle through a barbed wire fence. Some of them get bizarre tattoos or even brandings. Why? In a quest to be recognized, in a heartfelt desire for attention. Any schoolteacher can tell you that for an attention-starved child, any attention—even bad attention—is better than being ignored.

Young girls end up in the arms of the first boy who listens to them, who seems interested in them, who pays them some attention. Don't worry,

Dad, Mom, if you're too busy for your kids—Satan will find someone to give your daughter love. He will provide a man of the world or perhaps an experienced woman to answer your son's questions. The enemy of their souls will see to it someone is there to provide your children the guidance you are too busy to give. Like a wolf prowling around the edge of a sheepfold, Satan is always looking for a weak or neglected lamb to steal from the herd.

Chan Gailey, former coach of the Dallas Cowboys, is an avid golfer, yet he made a commitment that he would give up the game until his young boys were raised. As a Christian father, he concluded it was hard for him to justify spending four to six hours two or three times a week away from his growing boys. And he was right. He might not have won a Super Bowl with 'Da Boys' but you can bet he is an All-Pro dad with *his* boys! One hundred years from now, that is what will have mattered most.

*The family and public policy issues*

One of the saddest things I've witnessed in the last thirty years is how our government's policies have actually enforced Satan's attack on the family, the fundamental building block of society. As the family goes, so goes the nation. Yet many of our laws and court decisions have played right into the enemy's hands. Every one of the social and political issues we will examine in the chapters that follow stem from this onslaught against the family.

Abortion and euthanasia diminish the family by actually taking the lives of family members. The attempt to legalize homosexual marriage is a direct attack on God's design for the basic family unit. Education policies indoctrinate our children in political correctness, separate a child from his or her faith, and attempt to supplant the parent and child relationship.

The economic attacks on the family are mind-boggling. Liberal welfare policies have obliterated poor families. For every dollar our government spends on programs to reduce illegitimacy or support marriage, it spends about a thousand dollars subsidizing single parenthood.[4] Our income tax system imposes a penalty on married couples who file joint returns; it would be cheaper for them just to live together. More than once President Clinton has vetoed the attempts of Congress to overturn this marriage tax penalty. We need a president in office who will not thwart the efforts of the dedicated men and women in our federal legislature who are trying to relieve the heavy burdens imposed on families.

It is a tragedy that at the very time we are seeing the family structure crumble, with all its devastating consequences, those of us who are vocal in our support of "traditional family values" are objects of ridicule for the media elites and the mighty power brokers in Washington. I don't care what label the press or anyone else pins on me, I believe with all my heart that we can—and must—change the direction of our ship of state.

What follows in these pages is an overview of what I believe to be the most important issues we are facing as a society. And the number one issue on my list is abortion.

# 3  *Abortion: The Line in the Sand*

---

To weaken the church, to dilute the power of the gospel alive in each of us, to erode the structure of society from order to anarchy, Satan will stop at nothing. Abortion is one of his most sinister machinations: it strikes against the very heart and fiber of what a family is about. For the mother and father of a child to petition a doctor to extinguish its life goes against everything motherhood and parenthood represent. The abortion movement is nothing less than an attempt to foment social change, to "liberate" women from the obligations, cares, and responsibilities of motherhood.

Social liberals, who are really societal engineers, want to dissolve the traditional family structure. Therefore, childbearing—that most womanly of functions—represents everything the feminists and social revolutionaries want to eliminate. Thus the clamor for abortion. If a woman can have the option of sex without pregnancy, the thinking goes, then the woman is freed from the domination of man and from the obligations of home and family—and thus equally free to be a coal miner or lumberjack or oilfield hand.

It is beyond doubt that women are intelligent and capable of doing many of the same things men can—but there also are physical and emotional differences between men and women. That's why there is a ladies tee-box on every golf course and why female firefighters do not have to pass the same physical skills tests that male firefighters do. The abortion movement is but one manifestation of the rebellion of man against God's ultimate order for the structuring of society. Any woman who has a problem with so-called "domesticity" needs to read Proverbs 31—there you'll find a Supermom who had it all. The ideal woman presented in Scripture bloomed and flourished within the larger context of her family commitments and was a blessing in every way to all she loved. She had to be the most self-fulfilled woman in the entire Old Testament—and an example to all.

*A choice between light and darkness*

There is no larger issue in America today—no debate that more clearly draws the line in the sand between right and wrong—than abortion. It is a line that demarks a difference every bit as dramatic and obvious as the line between light and dark our astronauts see as they orbit the earth and pass from day into night and from night into day.

If you have ever gone down into a cavern and had your tour guide turn the lights off, you understand what the word *darkness* means. Before they cut off the lights, they always make certain you have a sure footing, because when they cut the lights it is as if the darkness explodes through the backs of your eyes into your brain. Then when the light is finally switched back on, the difference is more dramatic than anything you have ever seen—and your relief is palpable.

The difference we, as followers of Jesus Christ, are to make in the world should be as dramatic as turning on the light in the deepest, darkest cavern. We are "the light of the world" (Matt. 5:14), but we must remove our lights from under their coverings, and we must shine the light of God's love and the saving message of Jesus Christ into every dark corner of each of our worlds.

Ever since the misguided Supreme Court decision of *Roe v. Wade* in 1973, a war has raged between the forces of light—who stand for preserving the lives of the most innocent and defenseless among us—and the powers of darkness and evil—who in the name of "reproductive freedom" argue for the right to end the lives of children they deem to be an inconvenience. This, they say, is their "choice" to make.

What I'm going to say next may surprise you, but when it comes to abortion, I believe God is pro-choice. Now, before you conclude that I'm as nutty as a box of circus peanuts, let me show it to you in Scripture. Speaking through Moses, God told His people: "I call heaven and earth as witnesses today against you, that I have set before you life and death, blessing and cursing; therefore choose life, that both you and your descendants may live" (Deut. 30:19). God created us as free moral agents, with the capacity to choose our course of action. But He was quite explicit about what choice we should make: "choose life." Got that? *Choose life!*

Americans have *not* been choosing life in staggering numbers. Almost a million-and-a-half abortions are performed every year in the United States—well over thirty-seven million babies have been wantonly destroyed since our Supreme Court rewrote abortion laws nationwide.[1]

During the Vietnam War, every afternoon the newscasters announced the daily body count: how many dead, how many wounded. The loss of 55,000 American service men and women during the extended Vietnam "conflict" caused riots here at home, turned a generation of children against their parents, and drove a president from office.[2]

In the press today, however, you will seldom hear the body count in the battle against the unborn—and certainly not a daily report. Yet every two weeks in this country, the number of children murdered in the abortion mills

of America equals the number of U.S. lives lost in Vietnam. *Every two*

*weeks.* But there is no outcry in the press. No reporting about dead babies.

You only hear talk about and "unwanted tissue" and "termination of

pregnancy" and "reproductive freedom"—and quite a bit about "choice."

This never-before-discovered right to choose whether to carry a pregnancy

to term was a bit of legislating from the bench, a decision made by the nine

unelected—and unaccountable to the public—justices of the U.S. Supreme

Court. None of us got to vote on it, none of our legislators enacted it into

law, no previous constitutional scholars were aware of any such right until

the Supreme Court decided to make it the law of the land.


*Not quite a citizen*

*Roe v. Wade* was not the first Supreme Court decision to totally decimate the

civil rights of an entire class of people. In the years immediately prior to the

American Civil War, the Supreme Court decreed in *Dred Scott v. Sandford*

that a Negro was not as "human" as a white person and therefore could be

bought and sold as property. During World War II the Supreme Court

decided it was constitutional to disenfranchise Japanese-Americans of their

property and to intern them in what were basically concentration camps for the duration of the war. Those decisions, both *Dred Scott*, which sanctioned slavery, and *Korematsu v. United States*, which justified intèrnment of citizens on a racial basis legal, were terrible constitutional decisions. So was *Roe v. Wade*, which held, among other things, that an unborn child was not a person and therefore not protected by the Fourteenth Amendment to the Constitution. The Amendment says that a state shall not "deprive any person of life, liberty, or property, without due process of law; nor deny to any person within its jurisdiction the equal protection of the laws."

Justice Blackmun's majority opinion stated: "If this suggestion of personhood is established, the appellant's case, of course, collapses, for the fetus' right to life would then be guaranteed specifically by the Amendment." The court went on to say, however, that it was persuaded "that the word 'person,' as used in the Fourteenth Amendment, does not include the unborn."[3]

There, in a nutshell, are three strikes against the highest court in our country. *Dred Scott* was an outrage: no man should be allowed to own or to enslave another. *Korematsu* was a grievous injustice: no citizen should be discriminated against and locked up on the basis of ethnic heritage or the color of their skin. And *Roe v. Wade* is an abomination: no one should be allowed to kill another human, born or unborn, healthy or disabled, young or infirm—each should be allowed the maximum of "life, liberty, and the pursuit of happiness" that God in His sovereignty has chosen to afford them.

That no one should have the right to take the life of the unborn is an ancient principle of medicine. The Hippocratic Oath,[4] first formulated as a sworn rule of conduct for doctors and physicians in ancient Greece about 2,400 years ago, says, "I will give no deadly medicine to any one if asked, nor suggest such counsel; and in a like manner I will not give a woman a pessary to induce an abortion." Even then, four hundred years before the birth of Christ, people were clamoring for euthanasia and wanting to kill their unborn babies. If Hippocrates—a pagan physician who believed in all sorts of mythological gods, demi-gods, and goddesses—knew that it was wrong to take a life, what defense do we have today after the intervening two millennia of research and learning?

Abortion is nothing *but* "deadly medicine." It is nothing short of the deliberate, premeditated extermination of a living human being. Abortion is no less brutal than stomping a bug under your shoe—and it is every bit as final to the child murdered by the abortion doctor as it is for whatever insect you choose to squash.

Every school child learns these words from the pledge of allegiance: "One nation, under God, with liberty and justice for all." But for millions of children who never survived to be born a more appropriate statement would be "one unwanted fetus, under the abortionist's knife, with no chance for life and no justice at all."

Abortion ends a life—a human life—and it is as simple, and as wrong, and as hellish as that.

Abortion prevents a future teacher from teaching, it stops a future coach from leading, it keeps a future doctor from healing, it guarantees that a future writer will never get a chance to inspire. Abortion is not only a sin against the infant, abortion not only causes deep psychic scars in the aborting mother, abortion is also a sin against the future of humanity. Over thirty-seven million putative U.S. citizens have been legally murdered in this country.

Only God Himself knows how many presidents, how many athletes, how many ministers, how many mothers, and how many Nobel laureates have been put to death before they ever had a chance to make their contributions to humanity. It is quite possible that cures to cancer, AIDS, depression, and Alzheimer's have been delayed because the little boy or girl who would have grown up to make those discoveries was murdered in a mother's womb.

*Not quite born*

In the eyes of a majority of our Supreme Court justices, a human fetus is not yet a person and therefore not quite a citizen, and therefore it is permissible to "terminate" that life as long as it is not quite born. The insanity of the debate is epitomized in the recent Court ruling that gave constitutional sanction to a woman's right to have her full-term, fully gestated baby brutally murdered while it is the birth canal. I'm referring to the gruesome procedure known as a D & X (dilation and extraction) or partial-birth abortion. In his dissenting opinion in the case that overturned Nebraska's ban on this procedure, Justice Antonin Scalia called it a "live-birth abortion."[5]

In a moment, I will explain to you in detail this barbaric procedure whereby a doctor can now, in America, legally murder a *full-term infant.* But first I want to warn you that if you have a weak stomach, if you are the least bit easily nauseated, or if you have trouble sleeping because of things you might have seen or read, then please skip what follows—because what follows is so graphic, so horrific, that it will make a permanent impression on your mind.

---

*Warning!*

The following pages contain a graphic description of
partial-birth abortion. This is not suitable reading
material for young children or those who may be
easily disturbed by violence and brutality.

---

First, you must understand that we are not talking about a blob of
unviable fetal material—although the viability argument is irrelevant to me:
life is sacred, from the moment of conception to the utmost extremes of
senior citizenship. A partial-birth abortion is almost always performed on a
viable child,[6] usually a third-trimester fetus, quite possibly even a full-term,
completely gestated baby—a human infant that would be capable of living
outside the womb. We are talking about the premeditated termination, the
legalized medical execution, of a completely viable, completely adoptable,
living human infant. What we are talking about is sinful, it's wrong, and it's
every bit as repugnant in the eyes of God as when the ancient Canaanite
pagans threw their infants into the fires as living sacrifices to appease the
appetites of their demon god Molech (Lev. 20:2–5).

This D & X procedure has been labeled "partial-birth abortion" because the killing takes place *in the birth canal.* Because labor has not started naturally, the woman must undergo several days of painful dilation by the insertion of seaweed-type laminaria before this surgical procedure can be performed. Once the mother is sufficiently dilated, the doctor—correction: *the abortionist*—reaches inside the birth canal, feeling for the baby, endeavoring to grab hold of a little leg or arm or hand in order to present the child for a breech delivery (where the child exits the mother feet first, as opposed to a crown, or head-first, delivery).

When the baby's feet, legs, and arms are presented—which is to say that about three-quarters of the baby is dangling outside the mother, with the baby's face and head still not visible—the doctor literally has to halt the birthing in mid-process so as to physically prevent the mother from delivering a live baby into his hands.

Before I continue, let me point out that, as I understand it, for this procedure to be legal it is essential that the baby's head not be allowed to exit its mother's cervix until the abortionist has completed his murderous, bloody procedure. That means should the doctor look away and carelessly allow the mother's contractions to completely deliver the child, it would then be considered born, and termination of the unwanted "fetal material" could then legally be deemed murder.

So, with one gloved hand preventing the three-quarters delivered infant from continuing its journey through the birth canal, the abortion doctor reaches for a pair of razor-sharp surgical scissors. He rotates the child over and then places the scissors at the base of the baby's skull, where the head rests on the neck, and then rams the scissors home, severing the spinal cord. Poking the points of the blades directly up through the brain stem into the skull, into the brain itself, he plunges them deep into the baby's cranium, and the infant's blood spurts and flows out of its mother's womb much as the amniotic fluid did when her water broke.

Making sure of his grip, as little arms and legs dangle and thrash in panic as they protrude from the mother's birth canal like an arrangement of flowers violently spilled from a vase, the abortionist is careful to keep the child's violated head submerged in its agony within its mother.

The abortion doctor then works the scissors blades protruding from the back of the baby's skull, scrambling the dying child's brains beyond any possibility of reconstitution and making certain that he has completely severed the baby's brain stem, or *medulla oblongata*—what neurologists call the "primitive brain" because it is from there that all essential life functions are controlled. Then he inserts a suction hose—its medical name is a

*cannula*—into the baby's brain cavity, through the hole created when the

abortionist poked his scissors into the squirming infant's skull, and vacuums

the remaining slurry of brains and blood out of the dead child's cranium.

Once the brain cavity has been suctioned clean, the doctor collapses the

child's evacuated skull like an empty beer can. What remains of the child's

crumpled head is then allowed to exit the birth canal—and the baby is

discarded as biological waste, unless it is to be salvaged for biomedical

research or tissue harvest. [7]

It takes nine months inside a mother to get a child from the moment of

conception to the point of fully-gestated birth—it takes less than nine

seconds for an abortionist to plunge his scissors into that innocent child's

head and end its life on earth.

*A line in the sand*

I don't think God recognizes that last four inches of the birth canal as

making any difference as to whether this procedure is cold-blooded,

deliberate, premeditated murder or not. Whether inside the mother or not,

whenever someone plunges a scissors into the head of any child it is

butchery, it is barbarity, and it is a sin unto Almighty God.

As America enters into this third millennium since our Lord walked this earth, the systematic, legally sanctioned abortion of healthy babies is our great national shame. Unless we humble ourselves, call on God, and nationally repent of our evil ways, I fear for the future of this great nation.

Americans sat transfixed in front of our television sets from the end of December 1996 through the early months of 1997 as we watched, and wondered, in horrified outrage, at the barbaric murder of innocent little JonBenet Ramsey in Boulder, Colorado, wondering if in fact her parents had killed her. Yet every day, all across America, thousands of innocent children are premeditatedly murdered by their parents—in cold blood, with the assistance of a medical doctor and nurses no less—and yet it never makes the news, and so very few are outraged.

Here in San Antonio, in 1836, the most famous battle in the war for Texas independence took place. "Remember the Alamo!" was the rallying cry for the Texians as they fought for independence from Mexico—much as the thirteen British colonies in the New World had fought for their independence from England sixty years previously.

At an old fortified mission named the Alamo, approximately 180 Texians—men, women, whites, Latinos—were trapped, surrounded by the two-thousand-man strong army of General Santa Anna and cut off from supplies or support troops. Two weeks into the siege, the Texians were offered a surrender ultimatum from the opposing forces. The Mexican general said that if they would lay down their arms and surrender, they would be allowed to leave their compound and their lives would be spared.

Colonel William Travis, leader of the besieged forces in the Alamo, mustered his men in the courtyard in front of the old mission building. You can still visit where this happened here in San Antonio—it's a significant national historic landmark. Travis presented Santa Anna's ultimatum to the troops and then concluded his famous speech by scratching a line in the sand with his sword, instructing his men that those who wished to stay and fight, and most certainly die, should cross the line to join him. Those who wished to take advantage of General Santa Anna's offer, he said, should remain still, and they would be free to leave.

Every person in the Alamo stepped over the line. Jim Bowie, one of the heroes of that hopeless cause, wounded and stretcher-bound, had two men carry the litter he was laying on over the line. He was committed and devoted and willing to invest the totality of his existence on the outcome of the cause he believed in. Would that we had more Christians so devoted and sold-out to the cause of Christ today!

I retell this story to make this point. There is a line of demarcation drawn in the political arena today. And that line is drawn squarely down the middle of the abortion debate. On one side of that line—the side where conservatives are, where Ronald Reagan was, and where George W. Bush is today—is the side that stands for life. On the other side of the line—the side where liberals are, where Bill Clinton is, and where Al Gore is—is the side that stands for death. No matter how often they couch their crusade in terms of choice and rights and freedom, it is still a campaign for the death of innocent human life.

It is time for us as Christians to step over the line and to quit straddling. Taking a position is not always a popular thing to do. It is time for us to quit worrying about acceptability, popularity, and approval. It is time for us to fight, and to refuse to compromise, on matters of life and death. We stand at the same crossroads as ancient Israel, and God is saying to *us* today, "I have set before you life and death … therefore choose life" (Deut. 30:19).

In the upcoming presidential and congressional elections, each person who is a follower of Jesus Christ is also faced with a choice. How we vote will determine the composition of the U.S. Supreme Court for most of the next generation. How we vote can determine our future religious liberties as well as whether or not our national abomination of abortion will be permitted to continue unabated. I do not know what you might choose, but "as for me and my house, we will serve the Lord" (Josh. 24:15).

One major party presidential candidate is pro-abortion; the other has promised to do all he can to defend the rights of the unborn. Again, to my mind, there is the line drawn in the sand; there is the demarcation between light and darkness, between right and wrong. I cannot in good conscience—not as a Christian, not as a pastor, not as a man of God—vote for the pro-abortion Democratic Party or their pro-abortion candidate, Al Gore.

The next president of these United States will get to nominate and seek Senate approval for perhaps one to four justices to the Supreme Court—the Court that by the narrowest of margins has granted partial-birth abortion, indeed all abortions, constitutional status. To best frame the debate, to best impact the judicial philosophy that will decide the constitutionality of legislation, to best control the types of legislation that will be proposed, and to most completely affect the overarching judicial doctrines that will govern our American society for the next ten to twenty years, it is important that we work for—*and vote for*—God-fearing, moral candidates who will appoint

God-fearing, moral men and women to judgeships in every area of the U. S. judiciary.

Jesus said, "Let the little children come to me, and do not hinder them" (Matt. 19:14). How can we as Christians vote for anything less?

*A final word*

If you have had an abortion—if you have paid for an abortion—if you have urged someone else to have an abortion—you need to confess your part in that murder and ask God to wash the lingering traces of that sin from your heart. "You shall not murder" (Ex. 20:13 NIV) is one of the Ten Commandments—and that means abortion is sin. But it is only a sin, and it is not the unforgivable sin. Your sins are no challenge for God to forgive—but first you must humble yourself, acknowledge your wrong, and ask Him to make things right inside you.

And then you need to forgive yourself. If you are a woman suffering from the painful scars of abortion (post-abortion stress syndrome is now being recognized as a legitimate mental and emotional disorder that can be treated), please know that there are loving, caring Christian women who have been down the same road. They can help you put your past behind you so you can live in the joy and freedom of Jesus. Call your local crisis pregnancy center and ask for a referral to one of these groups.

And if you have voted for pro-abortion candidates, if you have campaigned for abortion rights, if you have been active in your opposition to the prolife movement, you also need to ask God to forgive you for your part in this great stain of organized murder that has been so endemic in our nation for almost three decades. Then, once you've made your peace with God, make a promise to your Savior and to yourself to do the right thing this year with your vote. Make your vote count for what is right—make your vote a vote for life.

*Vote like Jesus would!*

# 4 *Euthanasia: The Desire to Escape Suffering*

One of the most powerful weapons in the argument over emotionally charged political issues such as abortion and euthanasia is the manipulation of language. Attention is deflected away from reality—that abortion is the taking of an innocent human life, for example—by changing the language of the debate: abortion becomes merely the termination of a pregnancy, the removal of unwanted fetal tissue, and above all, it is a matter of personal choice. Casting the argument in terms of civil rights—abortion is a woman's right to choose—makes the reality of murder so much more appealing to the average citizen.

The same thing has taken place in the debate over euthanasia, which literally means "a good death." Euthanasia advocates are now calling the "right to die" the "ultimate civil liberty."[1] While its proponents refer to a "peaceful death" and "death with dignity," what euthanasia is really about is the desire to escape suffering. A person should not have to linger or suffer or live out the last days of life as an invalid or in pain, the theory goes; each of us should be able to determine when and how we die. There are several aspects to this debate, some relatively innocuous, others pregnant with eternal ramifications.

Christians, of course, do not welcome extreme suffering; we desire to escape it as much as anyone else does. Yet we recognize that suffering is sometimes an inescapable part of the human condition in our fallen world: pain, aging, and death are common to every man. We also know that the light of our testimony shines most brightly in the darkest of times. How a faithful, spirit-filled believer deals with the indignities of pain and suffering over the course of time can be a tremendous witness to unbelievers of the grace and mercy of God.

And above all, as Christians we understand that God is in control of our lives—and our death.

One of the largest questions each of us must face, and answer, in the process of our faith-walk with Jesus is, "How big is God—really?" Faith, the substance of things hoped for, the evidence of things not seen (Heb. 11:1), implies a component of trust—a complete trust in the midst of a "situational blindness" not unlike trusting that the highway department continued the road past the mountain curve you cannot see around. It is well and good to say you believe in God and that you trust Him. But claiming to profess a redemptive faith in a sovereign God requires a suspension of ego and necessitates a submission to the discipline of living consistently with a called-of-God lifestyle even when we least want to.

Writing from his prison cell to the church at Philippi, Paul said that the one thing he wanted in life was "to know Christ and the power of his resurrection and the fellowship of sharing in his sufferings" (Phil. 3:10 NIV). We all want to know that resurrection power in our lives—but how many of us long to enter into the "fellowship of suffering" with Christ? Could it be that we can't have one without the other?

When it comes to personal suffering, our example is Jesus, whose agony extended to sweating drops of blood in the Garden of Gethsemane. His commitment to complete the will of His Father, regardless of the personal cost, is the antithesis of opting for the easy way out of pain or difficulty by means of suicide (with or without the assistance of a physician).

And when it comes to the suffering of others, our example is the Good Samaritan, who came upon a man who had been sorely beaten and was in grievous physical condition. The man was suffering from exposure, had lost a lot of blood, was probably dehydrated and in shock, may have been delirious, and was completely unable to fend for himself. In fact, if the Samaritan had not nursed him back to health, no doubt he would not have lived another day; wild animals would surely have killed him if his injuries hadn't. The *Good* Samaritan was a consummate caregiver, not a "mercy killer"—he did not bash the dying man's brains out with a rock or slit his throat to allow him to pass humanely into eternity. Why? Precisely because the Good Samaritan's actions were motivated by eternal values.

People in great pain, or those under pressure from relatives who are ready to get things over with or who can't stand to watch the suffering, are not equipped psychologically or emotionally to deal with extreme mental duress during times of physical strain. For a physician to act in any way other than to alleviate a person's physical pain and emotional distress, for a physician to assist his patient out of a transitory situation with a permanent solution is wrong, wrong, wrong.

*Why people want the "right to die"*

Imagine you've worked your entire life, scrimped, saved, and done without to build something with your spouse, to maybe pass something along to your children and your grandkids—and then suddenly you are struck down by a debilitating disease that will not only take your life but is likely to deplete your family's assets and financial resources before you finally cross the veil into eternity. Driving the right-to-die debate are just such physical, financial, and emotional concerns as these. First is the fear that the physical suffering from a terminal illness will be unremitting; then there's the fear of becoming dependent on others for the most basic of life-functions, which is emotionally traumatic; and finally there is the fear that the financial burden of the illness will reduce the sufferer's family to poverty.

As president of the American Academy of Hospice and Palliative Medicine, Ira Byock opposes euthanasia. Yet, he says, "the crisis is real. Studies document that pain among the terminally ill is widespread and undertreated ... Making matters worse, our system financially punishes people for being seriously ill and not dying quickly enough. Illness threatens a family's source of income; medical treatment threatens its savings. All this can make assisted suicide seem a reasonable escape from inevitable agony."[2]

Dr. Byock advocates increased palliative care (medical treatment to adequately relieve the patient's pain) accompanied by counseling and social services to provide comfort to the dying and the soon-to-be bereaved family. But right-to-die advocates play on these physical, financial, and emotional fears to promote their cause.

The tragedy of euthanasia lies in the generally well-intentioned arguments that well-intentioned people are using to justify it. They boil down to two ideas: respect for autonomy (*It's my life;*

*let me decide how and when to end it*) and compassion (*I wouldn't want to suffer like that* or, as we often put it, *I wouldn't let my dog go through this—we'd take him to the vet*). These are deeply deceptive arguments, but they appeal to values that we hold dear.[3]

The notion of autonomy—*It's my choice when and how I die*—runs contrary to the sovereignty of God. Occasionally someone will speak jokingly of a person's death by saying, "His number was up." That's actually an accurate statement biblically. Psalm 139 says that God has numbered our days—He sovereignly determines our lifespan before we are even born: "All the days ordained for me / were written in your book / before one of them came to be" (v. 16 NIV). I don't want to go home to heaven before my number is up. Every day that I draw breath, I know that God has a purpose for me to be here.

Some believers have written the letters of their Christian witness largest in their last days of pain and tears. Faith untested by fire is faith untested. Faith that prevails in the face of incredible adversity can be both inspirational and contagious.

Jesus told us that the enemy of our souls—the thief—only comes around "to steal, and *to kill,* and to destroy" (John 10:10). And Peter wrote that "our adversary the devil walks about like a roaring lion, seeking whom he may devour" (1 Pet. 5:8). Satan would love to tempt the suffering believer to take the easy way out, to give up the struggle and end his life before the number of days God has ordained for him is complete. And Satan especially longs to tempt the unbeliever to end his life prematurely, before he can make a decision that would change his eternal destiny.

The debate over physician-assisted suicide begs the question of the sanctity of life and instead elevates human desire over subjection to divine will, and it places function ahead of human uniqueness.

Today a simple search on the Internet will provide you with instructions on how to kill yourself. People write articles, publish books, and form societies all dedicated to the proposition of terminating one's existence whenever pain or the cares of life or the anticipation of a bleak future seem more unbearable than whatever transitory pain might be incurred in ending one's life. To reduce the stigma associated with the word *suicide,* proponents refer to it as *self-deliverance.* However, know this. No matter how many there might be who align themselves against God and the sanctity of human life, giving a barbiturate-laced cocktail or a heart-stopping injection or placing a garbage bag over someone's head or gassing them with carbon monoxide is, indisputably, *murder*. It always has been, and it always will be.

## Physician-assisted murder

Quite often those who clamor for the right to die are not the persons who will be doing the dying but those closest to them. It's not that the sickly person wants to die—it's that the family members can't stand to see the patient suffer or can't handle the excruciating burden of caring for a terminally ill person. In a study of hospitals in the Netherlands, where assisted suicide and euthanasia have been legal for two decades, "doctors and nurses reported that more requests for euthanasia came from families than from patients themselves. The investigator concluded that the families, the doctors, and the nurses were involved in pressuring patients to request euthanasia."[4]

So what is to be the proper response of Christian friends and family members to the terminal illness of a loved one? The first consideration is the Sixth Commandment: "You shall not murder" (Ex. 20:13). *Assisted suicide is nothing more than assisted murder!* Murdering the sick has never been a Christian response to disease and suffering.

The Christian response is found in the book of James. "Is anyone among you sick? Let him call for the elders of the church, and let them pray over him"(5:14). Quite simply, we are to comfort, we are to work to meet their (and their family's) physical and emotional and spiritual needs, and we are to *pray*. Praying for God to put an end to a person's suffering by divine healing—even if that relief may only come through the ultimate healing of death and a future glorified body—is the appropriate response. And praying for *God* to end a person's anguish by taking the sufferer home to heaven is a far cry from taking it upon *yourself* to end that suffering.

What is sad is the endemic devaluation of human life we see in virtually every aspect of our secularized, insulated-from-any-mention-of-God society. First, we took God out of the schools—now we complain and wonder that our doctors and judges are living and performing their professional functions as though there is no God, as though there will be no eternity, as though there is nothing special about created-in-the-image-of-God man.

Physician-assisted suicide is a horrendous evil upon our land. And that evil has come to be epitomized by a particular physician whose name has become synonymous with death.

Dr. Jack Kevorkian, currently serving out a 10-to-25-year sentence in Michigan after being found guilty of second-degree murder for helping a patient with Lou Gehrig's disease kill himself with a lethal drug, has become the international poster boy for the euthanasia movement. In fact, Dr. Kevorkian's name has now entered the "digital lexicon" as a synonym for discontinuing a project. If you hear a webhead talking about needing to "kevork" something, what he means is that he needs to terminate or kill that project or idea.

Dr. Kevorkian, who earned the nickname Dr. Death during the Korean War when he photographed his patients' retinas at the moment of death, has killed, or helped to die, over 120 patients—many of whom were not suffering from fatal diseases. Several autopsies have shown no discernible disease at all, and others show that patients received a high dose of sedatives several minutes before the procedure and may have been asleep or unconscious when the lethal injection was administered.[5]

*Oregon's brave new world*

Oregon became the first state to enact physician-assisted suicide legislation. Since late 1997, when the Oregon Death with Dignity Act took effect, forty-three people have opted for self-destruction under the law's provisions.[6] Most people would be shocked to realize that instead of always working to preserve their patients' lives, many physicians in Oregon were helping patients end their lives—even before the new law became effective. "In a survey of Oregon physicians published in the *New England Journal of Medicine* last year [1996], 60 percent said they should be able to help some terminal patients die, and 7 percent admitted to having done so."[7]

Oregon is the only state at the present to allow physician-assisted suicides—and the Death with Dignity Act is currently on appeal to the U.S. Supreme Court—but the euthanasia movement, energized by their Oregon success, is attempting to reproduce their success elsewhere. A referendum on assisted suicide will be presented to Maine voters in the November 2000 election.

What can we expect if other states follow Oregon's lead? A look at what has happened in other countries will give us a clear picture of the impact of assisted-suicide laws.

In Europe, as the practice has become more prevalent, physicians have actually had to intervene, after their patients botched their suicide procedures, and finish the killing for them—deliberately ending the lives of persons otherwise alive and capable of unique self-expression.

One of the most alarming consequences is a certain inevitable progression that spreads like ever-widening ripples in a pond. In testimony before congressional hearings on the subject of assisted suicide, Dr. Herbert Hendin reported: "Over the past two decades the Netherlands has moved from assisted suicide to euthanasia, from euthanasia for the terminally ill to euthanasia for the chronically ill, from euthanasia for physical illness to euthanasia for psychological distress, and from voluntary euthanasia to nonvoluntary and involuntary euthanasia."[8]

The Dutch courts have ruled that mental suffering without physical illness justifies assisted suicide. A 1993 case cleared a psychiatrist of any wrongdoing "in assisting in the suicide of his patient, a physically healthy but grief-stricken fifty-year-old social worker who was mourning the death of her son and who came to the psychiatrist saying she wanted death, not treatment."[9] This court decision—indeed the entire Dutch experience—proves that you cannot limit physician-assisted suicide to the terminally ill and not even the physically ill, and you cannot limit the practice to voluntary euthanasia—because the foundational argument for euthanasia is that some lives are simply not worth living.

Where is it all heading? What is the ultimate end if this current disregard for the sanctity of human life continues? The ultimate result will

be that living, aware human men, women, and children will be "aborted"
(euthanized) against their will, without their consultation or approval,
whenever it is deemed impractical or wasteful of otherwise-needed resources
to keep them alive. Indeed, a 1991 government-commissioned study in
Holland showed that in over one thousand cases each year, "physicians
admitted they actively caused or hastened death without any request from
the patient."[10]

Yes, you read that right: *without any request from the patient.* That's
where it leads, and that's why we cannot afford to let a false notion of
compassion reign supreme in this political debate.

At its heart euthanasia, just like abortion, is no more and no less than a
different facet of a multi-pronged, coordinated attack of hell upon the home,
upon the family, and upon the structure of society itself. There is no
difference philosophically between killing an infant or euthanizing a senior
citizen—both end the lives of an innocent, and both unravel, from opposite
ends, the "three-fold cord"[11] that binds a family to each other and keeps
them connected to God.

*Man's Technology vs. God's Sovereignty*

The debate over euthanasia has intensified as technology has increased dramatically. Man now has the ability to interject himself with medical technology into the equation of life and death. Today we can keep people alive artificially— not just temporarily during surgery or in the intensive care unit after a traumatic accident or medical emergency to allow time for the body to mend itself and for proper bodily functions to resume—but we can keep lungs breathing and hearts beating long after the brain has ceased to live.

We have machines that will breathe for you when you can't breathe on your own. We have machines that will pump blood through your body when your heart has been removed from your chest so the doctors can replace or repair it. We have machines that will filter your blood for your kidneys. We have pacemakers to keep your heart muscle electrically stimulated in order to regulate a weak pulse—and they will also keep your heart beating long after the portion of your brain that is supposed to fire that muscle has been allowed to cease its function by God.

What I am saying is this: inside the human brain is that spark of life, what the ancients referred to as *spiritos*, that animates you and makes you who *you* are. It is now possible for doctors, using modern medical technology, to keep your heart beating and your lungs breathing long after your brain is dead and after that vital part of you that makes you *you*—your spirit—has gone to God.

This is a difficult subject—but in these days of an aging populace more and more of us will be facing these questions. If a person is unconscious, completely unresponsive, and if there is no discernible brain function—if our technology can ascertain no brain activity at all—then there is no reason to believe that person is alive.

If by unplugging a respirator forcing air into otherwise nonfunctional lungs a physician causes a dead brain's corpse to cease being oxygenated, that doctor has not killed the patient—nor have the patient's relatives killed their loved one. If a person's brain is already dead, incapable of maintaining essential bodily functions, and has been so for some time, then the air pumped into his body no more makes him alive than does the air pumped into a flat tire at a service station make the tire alive.

Withholding a feeding tube or switching off the life support of an unconscious, unresponsive, comatose invalid whose every second of existence is *completely dependent* on technology—with no hope of recovery of independent function or interpersonal interaction or any kind of creative expression at all—is not killing a person. It is merely removing man's technological capabilities from hindering the ultimate expression of the will of God for that patient's sojourn here on earth. That is quite a different thing from the act of killing someone whose brain is still possessed of neurons that function, a brain that keeps the heart beating, a brain that keeps the lungs pumping—all without outside electronic assistance or mechanical intervention.

Unfortunately, that distinction is not always made in the arguments surrounding euthanasia and physician-assisted suicide. There is, as the American Medical Association has pointed out, a "distinction between act and omission" when it comes to end-of-life care. Proponents of assisted suicide often "fail to recognize the crucial difference between a patient's right to refuse unwanted medical treatment and any proposed right to receive medical intervention which would cause death. Withholding or withdrawing treatment allows death to proceed naturally, with the underlying disease being the cause of death. Assisted suicide, on the other hand, requires action to cause death, independent from the disease process."[12]

Longsuffering: the least popular fruit

The apostle Paul described the character traits Christians are to develop in our spiritual walk as the "fruit of the Spirit." They are, specifically, "love, joy, peace, longsuffering, kindness, goodness, faithfulness, gentleness [and] self-control" (Gal. 5:22). Some modern Bible translations use the word *patience* instead of the term *longsuffering*. It sounds slightly less uncomfortable to talk about patience, I suppose, but longsuffering is an apt expression. To have patience means the possibility of suffering, sometimes for a long time, the indignities and injustices of life.

Whether you call it patience or longsuffering, it is a quality too few of us strive to possess. (I speak from experience here. I've been known to stand in front of the microwave and yell, "Hurry up!") And it is a quality that is often needed in abundance as we face the end of a loved one's life or perhaps our own.

Paul spoke of the grave and of the sting of death as being the "final victory" of sin (1 Cor. 15:54–56) over fallen man, but that we as believers have an ultimate "blessed hope" of resurrection with Christ and of reunion with our loved ones someday in heaven (Titus 2:13, 1 Thess. 4:18).

How can you be a living demonstration of faith and dependence on God if you cannot trust Him for sufficiency to get through each day of His intended natural span of life for you? How can you let your light shine if you are easily tempted into extinguishing your life—or the life of a loved one—once life seems to cease being a celebration and turns into a torturous tribulation?

Difficult decisions about end-of-life care should be made before you are in a situation of temptation requiring you to exercise judgment—that way there is no decision necessary, because your mind is already made up.

In Matthew 4 we read how the Holy Spirit led Jesus into the wilderness and how Lucifer subsequently tempted Him to turn rocks into bread, just as Jesus was completing a forty-day fast. Talk about stress! Most of us can miss one meal and think we're hurting. Forty days is a long time—and Satan knew that. He knew that Jesus, in His physical man, was painfully hungry, that there was nothing Jesus wanted in His body more than food at that moment.

That's when Satan's offerings are most effective: when he has an apparent solution to an immediate physical crisis—when rationalization and justification make compromise seem not only more palatable but also most reasonable. And that's what makes the rallying cry of "death with dignity" so attractive when people in the throes of an immense crisis of suffering are desperately seeking relief.

One of the women who has been associated with this ministry for a number of years is currently going through "the valley of the shadow of death" with her beloved father. Connie Reece, a professional who has committed the use of her writing skills to the advancement of the kingdom of God, has painfully watched her father endure multiple system atrophy, a neurological disorder that has gradually reduced him from being an incredibly capable, supremely self-sufficient, physical giant of a man who was the rock of his family and a friend and benefactor to all who knew him into being a dependent invalid. Now he is incapable of performing the smallest of basic life-tasks without assistance. Helping him to stand up from his wheelchair, take two steps forward and pivot a quarter-turn, then sit in his recliner can take up to five minutes of constant verbal cueing; his muscles no longer respond automatically to signals from his brain. Very soon, she fears, he will be bedridden.

Aside from her own pain—and grieving in advance at the certainty and perhaps the imminence of her father's death—Connie has had to be strong for her sister, a woman with physical challenges of her own; for her mother, who is watching the love of her life be reduced from protector and provider to dependent and recipient; and for her father, who is painfully aware that his debilitating disease is draining his family's resources even as he endures masculine shame, indignity, and frustration at suddenly being the weak link in his family's structure.

Here is a family who knows firsthand what it means to be forced to live with full faith and dependence on Jesus Christ, trusting that He still loves them even during these, the worst moments of a husband and father's life. They know what it means to pray for an end to suffering, to offer an anguished cry from the heart that God would hasten to take their loved one home to heaven. They are beginning to understand just what *longsuffering* can mean in the life of a Christian.

In the midst of all their misery, they find occasion to laugh as well as cry. One day recently Connie cried off and on all morning; she just wasn't coping well that day. Then she had lunch with her mom and dad, listened to him struggle to put into words the jumbled thoughts and images flashing through his short-circuiting brain, and they all got tickled at the absurdity of the situation. Afterward Connie sat down at the computer and wrote the following brief essay, full of humor and grace, about dealing with her father's decline.

If you, or someone you know, has recently lost—or is about to lose—a loved one, if you know someone with a debilitating disease, or if you're wondering how you can maintain your faith in the face of so many

seemingly unanswered prayers, then I encourage you to read (and share)
what follows.

### The Little People

I never thought I would find such humor

In the hallucinations of a dying man.

His body grows feeble, his brain withers

From the ravages of a cruel infirmity.

"Can you say 'neurodegenerative'?" I tease him.

"Not even when I was well," he replies.

Each day my father recounts for us

His adventures with the Little People.

He doesn't know what else to call

This myriad of unidentified beings

That populate his waking dreams.

He understands that no one else

Sees them or hears them—

Knows they are not real,

Yet is powerless to make them go away.

Only one of them ever speaks to him—

Steve, he calls their ringleader.

One night the Little People showed up

In Dad's bedroom at the usual hour.

"Go away," he told them. "I need my rest.

And don't come back for sixty days!"

The next night the Little People were back.

"I thought I told you to go away," he said.

"It's okay," Steve replied.

"We don't take up much room."

I guess that's why they're called the Little People!

Evidently wit does not reside at the neuronal level,

For my father has not lost his keen sense of humor

Even as the disease continues to destroy

His autonomic nervous system.

Or perhaps his ability to still crack a joke

Is simply a gift of God's grace

To a man and his caregivers,

Who have so little to laugh about

As we wait for the mercy of the inevitable.

When the time comes,

I'm thinking of asking Steve

To say a few words at the funeral.

I'd hate to exclude Dad's little companions

From the celebration of his voyage to heaven.


*Put feet to your faith*

How can you impact the euthanasia debate that is starting to make inroads here in America? Several ways. But first, and most dramatic, let me encourage you to seek to succor those in need, to invest some shoe leather in your application of the gospel. Learn about hospice care, which has for many proven to be the best treatment protocol to meet the needs of both the dying and their loved ones.[13] Better yet, sign up as a volunteer with your local hospice organization. Giving just a few hours a week of your time can help relieve the burden on a stressed-out caregiver who can't even leave a patient's bedside long enough to do the grocery shopping.

Christians aren't merely redeemed so that they might be saved—Christ also redeemed you that you might *serve.* There are any number of things you can do to help alleviate suffering at the end of a person's life. "People can be sat with, in quiet conversation or in silence.

They can be sung to, and their skin gently oiled. They can be prayed with."[14]

Such small gestures can be monumentally significant to a dying person.

Visit those in rest homes, volunteer to help those with shut-in loved ones (maybe allow them to have an afternoon or a few hours off)—do what you can to shine the light of Christian charity and compassion into lives Satan is trying to overwhelm with darkness and depression. If nothing else, you can go sit with a patient or their loved ones—nobody wants to die or watch their loved one die alone or forgotten. Live a life consistent with the gospel message—seek to be of assistance to those whose lives are radically impacted and constrained by pain, loneliness, and depression so that you infuse them with a greater desire for life and help them ascertain God's continuing purpose for their living.

Help prepare your family well in advance of any crisis. Ask your county medical society for information on preparing what are known as advance directives. You do not need an attorney to prepare a durable power of attorney for health care, which will appoint someone you trust to make medical decisions for you if you become unable to do so. If you have been diagnosed with a terminal illness, you may also want to prepare a Living Will, a document that will state your personal preferences regarding artificial life support and end-of-life treatment. Give a copy of these documents to each health care provider, and keep a copy for your family.

If you are a Christian doctor or nurse or health care provider, commit right now that you will never take part in, or assist in any way, the suicide of another person.

Write letters to opinion makers, political leaders, newspaper opinion pages, and the Supreme Court expressing your concerns and opposition to assisted suicide.

Donate money to the groups attempting to overturn Oregon's assisted suicide law and those opposing the Maine referendum coming up this November.[15]

Donate money to candidates who oppose assisted-suicide, and support them in their election bid.

*Vote like Jesus would!*

# 5 *Gay Rights: A Moral Wrong*

---

I was angered by news reports of a sad episode at the 2000 Democratic national convention; in my opinion, it should have gotten a lot more press coverage than it did. As part of the official opening of one of the convention sessions, a color guard presented the U.S. flag and a guest led the audience in the pledge of allegiance. For this particular session, a Boy Scout had been selected to lead the pledge. As he stood with his hand over his heart and spoke into the microphone, some of the delegates began to boo noisily from the convention floor. Thinking of how proud I would have been as a father if one of my sons had been chosen to lead the pledge of allegiance at a national event, I became furious when I saw the television footage from the event and heard the jeers leveled at this young man.

Why did these rude Democratic delegates boo him? Because the organization he represented excludes homosexuals from serving as scoutmasters. While the Boy Scouts do not ask any member or sponsor about his "sexual orientation," they have taken a strong stand against selecting an avowed homosexual as a role model for Scouts—and they've fought for the right to exclude homosexual scoutmasters all the way to the U.S. Supreme Court. (Not coincidentally, enrollment in scouting is at an all-time high as the organization has held firm in their moral convictions.)

In June 2000 the High Court ruled that the Boy Scouts have the "freedom of association" right to set membership standards that allow them to retain their ban against homosexual scoutmasters. But the Supreme Court decision did not put the issue to rest. Homosexual activists—many of whom are active in Democratic party politics—are outraged that the Boy Scouts do not consider them appropriate role models for molding young boys. While the rude convention delegates were booing the Scout who led the pledge of allegiance, a bill was lurking in Congress that would revoke the federal charter of the Boy Scouts.

The federal charter, which the Scouts have held since 1916, is largely symbolic; the organization receives no government funding. But a symbolic blow is what the activists had hoped to land against the Scouts. In September 2000 the Republican leadership in the House voted to suspend the rules and consider H.R. 4892, dubbed by its sponsors as the Scouting for All Act and touted as a civil rights measure, even though it had not been passed out of committee. The bill was overwhelmingly defeated when put to a vote as a pre-emptive tactic.

In alerting its constituents to the pending vote, the Traditional Values Coalition said, "This move to punish the Boy Scouts for its sincere effort to protect boys from potential child molesters is an affront to every American."[1] I couldn't agree more.

Throughout the Bible, without any hint of compromise, God makes it clear that homosexual conduct is not just wrong—homosexuality is an abomination. It is sin, plain and simple. Homosexuality and lesbianism are nothing more than perversions of God-ordained sexuality. The sexual libertines of our day long to redefine what the word *family* means. They hope to legitimize their status in society by changing the very fabric of how society is constituted.

Two men together cannot procreate, neither can two women; they cannot reproduce, only seduce. Yet homosexuals and lesbians are adopting children and raising them in conjunction with their same-sex roommates, and they want to define their collaboration as a family. Stanford Law Professor Michael Wald, quoted in the December 17, 1999, *Christian Science Monitor*, estimated that "there are 400,000 gay partnerships in California and many of these are families with children."[2]

What that means is that thousands, perhaps hundreds of thousands, of little boys and girls in California are being raised with two mommies or two daddies—or else with a woman called daddy or a man called mommy—and they are seeing their same-sex "parents" hug, kiss, and God only knows what else. These defenseless, impressionable young children are being indoctrinated that deviance is not deviant, that perversion is normal, that there is no shame, that there is no stigma in sin.

*Let's Get Our Definitions "Straight"*

Before I continue, we should define some terminology. My preference is to use the words *homosexual* and *lesbian*, although homosexuals prefer to call themselves *gay*. At times, in the course of this chapter, I will use the word *gay* in reference to homosexuality and lesbianism, usually because of the context of a particular source quoted herein. For convention's sake, whenever you see *gay,* it will mean *homosexual* and *lesbian* (and unnatural, abominable perversity); nonetheless, to me, as a student of traditional English, it is queer to use the word *gay* in reference to a homosexual lifestyle.

Let me tell you from many years of personal ministry experience that homosexuality (by which I include any same-sex relationship, male or female) is not a supremely happy or carefree lifestyle. That's what the word *gay* used to mean, and I'm angry about the loss to the language of a great word. Some of you with gray in your hair will probably remember that *gay* used to be the highest expression possible of lighthearted happiness. In fact, it used to be a name people would give their children. Not anymore.

When I was younger, homosexuals were referred to as being *queer* because that's what society acknowledged their lifestyle as being. Look the word up in an older dictionary sometime; the definition for *queer* exactly describes the "gay" lifestyle: strange, odd, peculiar, acting or behaving in a way that is not normal.

*Not normal.* That's why homosexuals don't want to be labeled as queer, and why that word has become so politically offensive. Above all, homosexuals want normalcy, acceptance, and equivalence with heterosexuals. Satan being the father of liars, he does not want the truth told about his demonic perversion of family sexuality; instead he offers a lie, a perversion that twists "not normal" into "happy and carefree."

Some gay rights advocates like to point out that the Bible does not mention the word *homosexuality*. But it couldn't—the word *homosexual* (*homo* + *sexual*, meaning "one- or same-sex") is derived from Latin root words that originated a thousand years *after* God, speaking through Moses, instructed in Leviticus 18:22, "You shall not lie with a male as with a woman. It is an abomination." You don't have to use the word *homosexual* to describe the conduct proscribed in that verse; the Bible paints a word picture so clear that no one can fail to see it.

The only word for homosexuality in the Bible was *sin*—no other reference was needed. When someone was caught in what we today call "homosexuality," they were taken to the outskirts of town and stoned to death.

### Striving for Normalcy Through Indoctrination

V.I. Lenin, founder of the atheistic, communistic Union of Soviet Socialist Republics, once said, "Give me a child until he is five years old and I will own him for life." Gay rights advocates and liberal educators similarly understand the importance of controlling the conditioning process that occurs in the schoolhouse.

The Bible says that if you "train a child up in the way he should go ... when he is old he will not depart from it" (Prov. 22:6). Many a parent has held onto that verse when a child has wandered away from his spiritual heritage. But that principle is not only true for good things, it also can apply to bad things. The Bible also speaks of generational sins, saying that "the sins of the fathers" can be passed down even "to the third and fourth generation" (Ex. 20:5). That speaks of parents teaching their children wrong behavior by example as well as indoctrination, thus passing their sins—and the consequences of their sins—from one generation to the next.

How are classroom activists trying to twist and contort our children's values and thinking into acceptance of homosexuality and lesbianism as valid lifestyles? "First and foremost, teachers must act promptly to stop anti-gay comments at their first appearance, explaining to children why they are wrong, and that there is nothing wrong with being gay. Students who persevere need to be disciplined or suspended to show children and their parents that the schools are serious."[3]

This is not something that is targeted toward only the younger students, either. At older ages, at that time of life when a youngster starts casting about looking for role models and making education choices to bolster career and values orientations, "pro-homosexuality teachers are using their position to 'mainstream' homosexuality in the classroom. In high schools and colleges, the main tactic has been to stress that famous historical figures were 'gay,' even if there is no definitive proof for the claim."[4]

Recidivist history alone not being deemed sufficient, homosexual activists are now trying to take the virtues of non-prejudice and open-mindedness toward people and twist those admirable attributes into liabilities. The concept of civil rights is being blurred from respecting all persons, regardless of race, creed, gender, or national origin into equating sexual orientation or sexual preference with color—i.e., homosexuals and lesbians should be accorded the same legal protections and benefits of the doubt that society accords to *oppressed minorities*.

"Homosexual education activists ... of GLSEN (Gay, Lesbian and Straight Education Network) claim to respect biblical beliefs but assert that all children must be taught to live in a diverse world in which "gays, lesbians, bisexuals and transgenders" are part of the mix.[5]

Yet while Christian students cannot have school prayer or school-funded Bible clubs, in Massachusetts there are taxpayer-funded homosexual youth clubs at schools.

Another central component of the "gay" education agenda is the formation of school-based "Gay-Straight Alliances" (GSAs), which are *de facto* homosexuality booster and propaganda clubs. In Massachusetts, where GSAs are taxpayer-funded, over one-half of about 300 public high schools host the clubs, which seek to combat "homophobia" and generally advance homosexual activist ideology. Every year, the Commission on

Gay and Lesbian Youth helps bus "gay, lesbian, bisexual and transgender" students from across the state to Boston for a pro-homosexuality pep rally on the steps of the state capitol.[6]

To make matters even worse, if such a thing could be imagined, there appears to be a growing trend for young people to be "encouraged to embrace a 'gay' sexual identity by their school counselors. The American School Counselor Association now endorses the claim of a natural and 'unalterable' homosexual identity for *sexual minority* (emphasis added by author) youth."[7]

It does not take very much research at all into the subject to figure out that "homosexual activists seek to displace the moral and religious teachings of parents about sexual morality with their own doctrine—revolutionary in the light of history—that homosexual relationships are as natural and valid as normal relationships between men and women."[8]

*Striving for Normalcy Through Acceptance*

There are only two nations on the planet right now that have fully legitimized homosexual marriages: Denmark and the Netherlands.[9]

However, several other European countries allow gays and lesbians to apply for registered partnerships, giving them many of the rights and obligations enjoyed by heterosexual married couples.

Much closer to home, in British Columbia, Canada, the provincial government

> offers gay and lesbian couples the same rights as heterosexual couples living in "common-law" relationships. A recent decision by the Canadian Supreme Court ordered the Ontario provincial government to change its legislation to recognize alimony rights of same-sex couples in a way that is identical to heterosexual common-law couples ... (Canadian) Gay and lesbian groups ... identified 38 federal laws which gave special privileges to heterosexuals and denied the same rights to gays and lesbians ... In 1999 ... the (Canadian) government announced that it will shortly change all 38 laws to grant all Canadians equal treatment.[10]

At issue in the whole debate over same-sex marriages is not property rights or the right to be able to live together or the right to be considered a couple. The trouble with settling for a registered partnership, as homosexuals see it, is that it offers "unequal treatment, is not recognized by other countries and is, in reality, a second class status. Many other countries provide various degrees of domestic partner benefits, but nothing close to the full, equal right of legal marriage. It is only by challenges to the legal exclusion of same-sex couples that marriage will become available."[11]

It is moving away from that "second-class" status that motivates homosexual advocates to push for removal of all legal exclusions protecting the traditional definition and framework of marriage as being that of one man and one woman. The clamor for same-sex marriages is not because homosexual men can't live together or because lesbian women cannot set up joint households—because they can and they have. The reason homosexuals and lesbians are fighting so vociferously for the right to marry is that they are seeking social legitimacy. What they are fighting for is legal equivalency. What they aspire toward, instead of forsaking their sin and repenting and turning to God, is full acceptance and endorsement of their sin.

*Attempts to Legalize Homosexual Marriages in the U.S.*

It is not for a lack of trying that homosexuals have not achieved the right to marry here in the U.S. Here is a brief review of attempts to legalize homosexual marriages: [12]

- In 1975, the City Council of Washington D.C. considered, but did not enact, a bill permitting same-sex marital unions.

- In 1984, Berkeley, California, became the first city to extend spousal benefits to same-sex live-in partners of city employees.

- In 1987, the ACLU (American Civil Liberties Union) committed to work toward eliminating legal barriers against same-sex marriages.

- In 1989, the San Francisco Bar Association issued a statement in support of same-sex marriages.

- In 1990, a bill was filed in the California state legislature to permit same-sex marriages (the bill was endorsed by the

California Bar Association and the Bar Association of San
Francisco).

• In 1993, in Texas, State Representative Glen Maxey
introduced a bill to extend equal marital rights to same-sex
partners. It did not get out of committee.

• In 1996, a bill was introduced in Nebraska to legalize same-
sex marriage—it failed.

• In 1997, another legislative attempt was made in
Nebraska—it, too, was defeated. Legislation to sanction same-
sex marital unions was also introduced in the states of
Maryland, Wisconsin, Oregon, and Washington—all were
defeated. In Hawaii, legislators instituted a "Reciprocal
Beneficiaries" law that offered 50+ benefits to same-sex
couples; also, the Hawaii legislature passed a constitutional
amendment that stated: "The legislature shall have the power to
reserve marriage to opposite-sex couples."

• In 1998, Maryland again had a bill to legalize same-sex marriages introduced—again, it failed. In Rhode Island, a bill to legalize same-sex marriages was proposed.

• In 1999, in Rhode Island, legislation was introduced to secure legalized status for same-sex marriages. In Vermont, the state legislature made provisions for "Civil Union" for same-sex couples. A "Civil Union" is not the same as a marriage, but it does offer a range of protections for same-sex couples never before available in the United States.

The above listing was excerpted from a single website, a pro-homosexuality site at that, and should not be considered exhaustive.

To halt the move toward legitimization of same-sex marriage, a number of state legislatures have passed measures (or, in the case of California, a voter referendum) defining marriage as a heterosexual union and refusing to recognize same-sex marriages that might be performed in another state. Since 1995, more than thirty states have adopted these so-called "defense of marriage" laws.

In 1996, a federal Defense of Marriage Act became law. Introduced

by Representative Steve Largent, a Republican from Oklahoma, it defined

the term marriage within federal law as encompassing "*only a legal union*

*between one man and one woman as husband and wife.*" The act also

excused each state from having to follow the "full faith and credit" clause of

the U.S. Constitution, thus allowing one state to refuse to recognize a

marriage made in another state if the spouses were of the same gender. A

similar bill was introduced in the Senate by Senator Don Nickles of

Oklahoma. Both houses of Congress passed the bill with a huge majority,

and it was later signed into law by President Clinton as it seemed almost

certain that a veto of the pro-family legislation would be overturned by the

Senate. The Federal Defense of Marriage Act of 1996 stipulates "that while

states could determine for themselves what constitutes marriage, when it

comes to federal matters the U.S. government would only recognize

marriage as being between a man and a woman."[13]

In California, on March 7, 2000, voters passed Proposition 22, which

stated that California will recognize only those marriages that are between a

man and a woman, making California the thirty-first state to make sure

marriage remains traditional.[14] But that won't be the end of the matter. In a

newspaper feature published three months prior to the vote, a Stanford

University law professor stated that the upcoming referendum was "just part of a 10- to 15-year discussion that, in an historic sense, is really just beginning."[15]

Marriage has always been recognized as a special relationship, something beyond mere friendship, and something that always existed between a man and woman who commit to each other in a lifelong contract, instituted by God, covenanted to in His presence, and recognized by government and society.

Society, through government, has an interest in encouraging marriage and in preserving its uniqueness under law. "In the United States today, each state governs its own marriage laws. The legal provisions themselves number into the hundreds in each state, and more than 1,049 on the federal level. These laws cover almost every conceivable aspect of social interaction."[16]

One aspect of U.S. law is that, under the Constitution, states are not allowed to legislate against each other, to impose selective tariffs, or to restrict interstate commerce among the states. How that applies to marriage is that "Article IV, Section 1 of the U.S. Constitution states that 'full faith and credit shall be given in each state to the ... judicial proceedings of every other state.' Thus, if one state legalizes same-sex marriages, and a couple is married in that state, then the remaining 49 states are required to recognize the marriage."[17]

It is a sign of our troubled times, a proof that we are in what Jesus called the "last days," that legislators are having to enact laws spelling out the obvious: that marriage is a unique covenant between a man and a woman. Why is this happening? Because the forces of darkness, in their unending assault on the family, are seeking to redefine away the uniqueness of the family unit to where any group of people could seek the legal protection of family status.

If Satan can destroy the family, if he can erode away the societal foundations that undergird the traditional upbringing of children, then he can capture the next generation. That is why concerned people across America have worked to have their legislators and representatives—in thirty-one states at last count—to pass laws specifying that marriage shall be constituted only of one man and one woman. These Defense of Marriage Acts are being passed because godly people in each of those states have taken action to protect their children and to insulate their families from any legislative inroads the forces of unrighteousness might realize in any of the other states. The current thinking is that the best thing to do is prohibit same-sex marriage *before* it becomes legal somewhere else. These measures are being passed to help protect against the imaginations of liberal judges whose agendas might include accomplishing by judicial *fiat* what their fellow travelers are unable to get enacted by popular legislative ballot.

It is vital that no state legalize "same-sex" marriages—ever. In the nineteen states where no Defense of Marriage Acts have been enacted, concerned Christians should contact their legislators and let them know that traditional morality and family uniqueness is important to them—so important, in fact, that it will affect how they complete their ballot next election. In the thirty-one states that have adopted a Defense of Marriage Acts, it is important that legislators and public officials be elected who will commit to maintaining the sanctity of the marriage relationship.

In all fifty states it is essential that Christians register, make their views known—both to their family and friends as well as to their candidates and public officials—and that they *VOTE Like Jesus Would!*

# 6 *Education: The Necessity of a Moral Foundation*

It used to be in America that moral values and a belief in the absolutes

of right and wrong were part and parcel of an American education. Whether

it was a young child learning to read from a McGuffy Reader or a teen or

young adult preparing for a professional career at an American college,

certain concepts of morality were considered to be fixed and timeless—an

immovable foundation to build one's life upon. In fact, "right up to the end

of the nineteenth century, the most important course in an American

student's college career was moral philosophy, or what we today call ethics.

The course was seen as the crowning unit in the senior year, usually taught

by the college president himself. As President James Monroe said of such

classes, 'The question to be asked at the end of an educational step is not

"What has the student learned?" but "What has the student become?"'"[1]

Indeed! "What has the student become?" What has become of our

students? Why is there a lament in the land that so many of our children,

raised in the knowledge of the Lord, go off to college and come home with

doubts about the efficacy of their faith, questioning whether Dad and Mom might not be a little behind the times for the values they continue to insist their children uphold.

Former Harvard University President Derek Bok, in his 1986–87 report to his university's Board of Overseers, repeatedly made the point that universities should help students learn how to lead ethical and fulfilling lives, yet he admitted that the faculty are not equipped to teach morality and absolute values. After all, you cannot draw water from a well that has no water in it. Specifically, Bok wrote, "Professors ... are trained to transmit knowledge and skills within their chosen discipline, not to help students become more mature, morally perceptive human beings."[2]

When schools do bother to teach what they call "ethics," it is not what our parents and grandparents meant when they talked to us about right and wrong. The sad reality is that "much of today's focus is on 'prevention ethics' rather than on principled ethics. It is more concerned with 'not being caught' (or sued or exposed in the press) than with doing right."[3] We have only to look at the White House to see a prime example of such ethics. Under legal questioning, the president of our nation debated the definition of the most basic verb in the English language: *is*. In his eyes, he was only guilty of serious misconduct if you failed to follow his convoluted word play.

In his brilliant work, *Time For Truth*, contemporary Christian thinker Os Guinness explained our current educational disaster in one sentence: "The fruit of the Western universities in the last two hundred years has been to destroy the possibility of any moral knowledge on which to pursue moral formation."[4] He went on to say, "Technologically Western civilization has advanced into the age of space and cyberspace, but ethically we have regressed. 'We have been thrown back,' Christina Sommers writes, 'into a moral Stone Age; many young people are totally unaffected by thousands of years of moral experience and moral progress.'"[5]

Mere knowledge without moral values and an appreciation for God's rules for life and living is as dangerous as a loaded pistol or a rotating chain saw in the hands of a young child. Asking anyone, adult, child, or college student, to try to navigate the moral morass of modern society without absolute standards of truth, morality, and conduct would be like asking a city person to find their way through the wilderness in the black of night without a map, a flashlight, or a compass. Without absolute, objective directions, people lose their way—even trying their very best. That is why Jesus told his followers to let their light shine before men—to show them the way.

We should tear down the fancy nameplates over the administration buildings and write Ichabod ("the glory has departed") over the doors of most of our big-name colleges, for they have abandoned their foundations.

The American university system was built on a foundation of evangelical Protestant colleges. Most of the major universities evolved directly from such nineteenth-century colleges. As late as 1870 the vast majority of these were remarkably evangelical. Most of them had clergymen-presidents who taught courses defending biblicist Christianity and who encouraged periodic campus revivals. Yet within half a century the universities that emerged from these evangelical colleges, while arguably carrying forward the spirit of their evangelical forebears, had become conspicuously inhospitable to the letter of such evangelicalism. By the 1920s the evangelical Protestantism of the old-time colleges had been effectively excluded from leading university classrooms.[6]

Quite a few of the leading universities in our country today, especially in the Ivy League, were founded as Bible colleges and were headed by men of God. The founders of these schools were men who "were shaped by their strongly Protestant heritage. Most of the first generation of university builders were active Protestants and many were ardent believers ... until the early 1960s, almost all the leaders of the pace-setting institutions were of Protestant stock, had outlooks shaped by a Protestant ethos, and on occasion would honor their Christian heritage."[7]

What happened in the early 1960s? We took God out of the schools, we took the Ten Commandments off the walls, and it became illegal to teach a religion-based morality—instead educators taught our children that they were descended from apes by way of slime and that when they died, that was it. Adrift without foundations, a generation of students was ready to recite LSD guru Timothy O'Leary's mantra: "turn on, tune in, and drop out." The consequences of isolating the classroom from a religion-based morality have been absolutely devastating to society.

*Rewriting the Past*

Today *diversity* has become the buzzword of the political left. No matter what centuries of wise men have deemed right or true or proper for a youth's education, the trend these past several decades—a trend which has only accelerated under the Clinton-Gore administration, the so-called

"Education Administration"— is to weed out the traditional western philosophies and Judeo-Christian heritage generations of school children have been taught, in order to make other cultures equally significant, regardless of their actual contributions. Traditional educational resources have been set aside in recent times to remove what is considered the "white, European, male bias" from the educational curriculum. Their works have been replaced with the writings of blacks, Hispanics, women, and Asians merely because such authors are *not* white, European males.

As an example, one elementary school textbook devoted only a few pages to its discussion of World War II. No mention was made of Pearl Harbor, of Hitler's treachery, of the courageous British pilots, or any number of important aspects of this critical time in history. Instead, the textbook implied it was wrong for the A-bomb to be dropped, ending the war early and sparing over a million American and Japanese lives. The brief presentation of World War II did include, however, sidebar features on a black, a Latino, and a woman. Audie Murphy, General Eisenhower, General Patton, Admiral Nimitz, Winston Churchill, Charles DeGaulle—none of the real heroes of the war were discussed. The result was nothing but a sanitized account that reprioritized and retold history to suit the social agenda of liberal, One-World-minded educators.

I can remember from my own educational days that whenever there would be a change of government in Soviet Russia, the new people in power would rewrite their country's history and even reissue old photographs with the faces of the people out of power or out of favor blacked out. I would never have thought that could ever happen in America, but that is exactly what is happening today when textbook authors rewrite history in order to make it more "inclusive."

Such tactics remind me of the definition of a man who is "basically honest": that's a man who only lies when he has to.

I am as nonprejudiced as any man on earth, but I must tell you, recidivist history, rewriting past events to make them relevant to current political concerns, is wrong. It was *not* the United Nations that won World War II, it was the arsenal of democracy, the United States of America; the United States did not start the war, we ended it. And our history books ought to reflect that.

At the same time our educators are pushing for diversity, they have removed any notion of individual accomplishment in the classroom. One of my writing staff has a young daughter who attended one of the best elementary schools in the state. Every year the school would have a field day, and each child was allowed to compete in three events. At the end of the day, each child received three award ribbons: a blue first-place ribbon, a red second-place ribbon, and a yellow third-place ribbon. It didn't matter whether a student won, placed, or finished last—each student got exactly the same ribbons and recognition.

My employee didn't know this was the routine, so at the end of the day when he saw his little girl had finished either first, second, or third in every event in which she had competed, he was excited and congratulated her. His daughter responded, "It's no big deal, Daddy. Everyone got the same ribbons."

Individual achievement was forfeited for the sake of generating a false sense of self-esteem in the children. But the kids weren't fooled—only the adults were. Rewarding everyone deprived the individual of significance, and the students figured that out for themselves. What good is an award if it is mandatorily assigned to everyone? Those school administrators—although well-intentioned, like most social engineers—had reduced a little girl's prize ribbons to a significance of little more than a cash register receipt at the grocery store: it's no big deal, everyone who goes through the checkout aisle gets one.

Children need to learn the ethic of work and they need to experience recognition as a reward earned for genuine achievement.

## The Task of Education

School textbooks are like the tires on your car. You take them for granted—until you have a failure. And then everything stops as you literally might have to reinvent the wheel. In spite of being led for eight years by a man who can't define the word *is*, most people understand that words do have definite meaning. What is more, "ideas have consequences. Differences make a difference. Behavior follows beliefs as surely as thunder follows lightning. What starts in the studies will end in the streets."[8]

One of the greatest deceits of the enemy of our souls has been the notion that our Constitution forbids any mention of the name of God or Jesus in our public classrooms. That prohibition simply does not exist—it is nowhere to be found in the Constitution. The much-vaunted wall of separation between church and state is not a constitutional formulation. The phrase *wall of separation* does not come from the U.S. Constitution. It is not in the Bill of Rights, nor is it in the Declaration of Independence. So where did the phrase come from that many of our recent Supreme Court decisions are based upon? It was excerpted from a letter written by Thomas Jefferson to one of his friends when Jefferson was serving as John Adam's Secretary of State. That writing should have no more legal precedent than Martha Washington's grocery list.

What has happened, however, is that anti-God forces in our country, pandering to the interests of fallen men who desperately want there not to be a God so they can continue in their selfish spiritual rebellion, have seized upon that phrase by Jefferson. "Only in the past half-century or so has the phrase 'the wall of separation of church and state' been elevated from a remark in Thomas Jefferson's correspondence to virtual constitutional status. Some Supreme Court Justices invoked it as the basis for their decisions and the phrase became a slogan for those who wished to insulate public life from direct religious influence."[9]

The far-reaching nature of the impact of the exclusion of God, absolute values, and Bible-based morality from the entire spectrum of the educational curriculum cannot be exaggerated.

C. S. Lewis, one of the great thinkers and writers of the twentieth century, was also an educator. A collection of Lewis's essays, published as *The Abolition of Man* was primarily concerned with elementary education textbooks. Lewis believed that the process of conditioning students away from absolute values started at a very early age. And yet, he said, the task of education should be "to train in the pupil those responses which are in themselves approprate, whether anyone is making them or not."[10]

Eminent Catholic theologican John Henry Cardinal Newman was concerned with the other end of the business of teaching, the *university*-level curriculum. In *The Idea of a University,* Newman wrote about the then-current trend of college educators to drop theology, the science of the study of God, from college curricula. He argued that "as to the range of University teaching, certainly the very name of University is inconsistent with restrictions of any kind ... a University should teach universal knowledge."[11] Sounding almost prophetic of our day, Newman concluded that "if you drop any science out of the circle of knowledge, you cannot keep its place vacant for it; that science is forgotten; the other sciences close up, or, in other words, they exceed their proper bounds, and intrude where they have no right."[12]

What Newman meant, and accurately forecast, was that if you leave obvious truth like the existence of God out of the curriculum, other topics are going to suffer a natural exaggeration to fill in the gap left by the omitted theological truth. When you consider the school curricula of our present time, at every level of education—from preschool through graduate school—unless a student is attending a Christian private school or Bible college, God has been scrupulously and deliberately excluded from the textbooks. As a result, honest science has of necessity been distorted by anti-God, biased educators into a dishonest parody of itself in a limping attempt to fill the gaping chasm caused by their preclusion of God.

While diversity is promoted, one thing *not* being taught today in our public schools are differences: the differences between right and wrong, the differences between immorality and morality, and the differences between truth and untruth.

It is no longer acceptable to point out differences. That's what the political-correctness group-think effort is about: eliminating acknowledgment of differences. Freedom of speech is now freedom of speech only if conservative or evangelical values are not under discussion. Our children are being trained to think in terms of "world citizenry"—not as being Americans; they are told they are children of "Mother Earth"—not human beings uniquely created by God in the image of God. Our children are being trained to think in terms of "uni-sex"—with no preference given to heterosexual, male-female relationships; our children are being told that the word *family* means "any group of people who love or care for each other." Bonds of blood and marriage which have for millennia served as the definition of family are being derogated and discarded as archaic, limiting, and discriminatory.

Yet differences *do* matter to God—and if we are God's people, then those differences should matter to us. And we need to take care our children are properly educated to discern the difference between right and wrong, moral and immoral, good and evil, temptation and opportunity. Back before the Supreme Court took God out of the school curriculum, our children were taught not only what to do, but what to avoid. Educators used to not only dispense knowledge, they also inculcated wisdom and an understanding as to how best to utilize new information.

One of my favorite analogies about educating students comes from C.S. Lewis. He wrote that "the old (form of education) dealt with its pupils as grown birds deal with young birds when they teach them to fly: the new deals with them more as the poultry-keeper deals with young birds—making them thus or thus for purposes of which the birds know nothing. In a word, the old was a kind of propagation—men transmitting manhood to men: the new is merely propaganda."[13]

"As the poultry-keeper deals with young birds"—what a chilling image. The poultry-keeper does not love or nurture his birds, the poultry-keeper does not prepare young birds to thrive; he breeds (and culls) them to be cogs in his agricultural machine. But the old birds, to continue with Lewis's imagery, teach the young birds how to fly and fend for themselves, how to live independently, flying from tree to tree, not merely to live a life of programmed conformity in a coop.

The major difference between educators today versus educators in times past, Lewis said, is that "in the older systems both the kind of man the teachers wish to produce and their motives for producing him were prescribed by (Revealed Wisdom/God's Law)—a norm to which the teachers themselves were subject and from which they claimed no liberty to depart. They did not cut men to some pattern they had chosen. They handed on what they had received; they initiated the young neophyte in to the mystery of humanity which overarched him and them alike. It was but old birds teaching young birds to fly."[14]

Our education system today has lost that concept of propagation, as Lewis described it, in favor of propaganda. That is why we need changes in education—we need educators who live constrained, in discipline, to absolute morality and truth even as they seek to impart that discipline and fidelity to moral values to the children we entrust to them in our schools.

Along with losing sight of the purpose of teaching moral values, our schools have abandoned the discipline of students. When most of my generation were in school, if you got in trouble in the classroom, you got licks—usually from the principal or perhaps the football coach. And when your parents found out you'd gotten licks at school, your father finished the job when he got home from work.

Nowadays, not only are principals often prohibited by school district policies from administering corporal punishment, they are often hamstrung from expelling troublesome youths to prevent their distracting the other students who are attending school to learn. We've come to the place that teachers are now required to attend seminars on liability and are encouraged to carry personal liability insurance in case an irate parent wants to accuse them of discrimination or abuse or unfairness or humiliating their child. "Many educators fear legal recourse for applying even the mildest punishment for bad behavior. Moreover, student handbooks like 'Up Against the Law' and 'A High School Students' Bill of Rights' advise students that 'you don't have to answer a school official if he questions you,' and 'a teacher can't make you do anything that violates your conscience.'"[15]

When we are advising students of their rights to disobey and be disruptive, it seems to me we have abandoned any hope of significant educational accomplishment.

*The Importance of Leadership*

When I was a child, the president of the United States was the number one American. He had the top job in the country and was generally held to be one of the best our nation had to offer. That's not the case anymore, and our children are getting conflicting messages. Liberal teachers at school laud and praise their leftist fellow traveler Bill Clinton even as godly parents at home try to tell their children that lying is wrong, that sexual relations outside marriage are wrong, and that "spin" is untruth.

Lying *is* a big deal. I believe a person who will lie to you is capable of anything. Lying is like acid to the fabric of any relationship of trust. Lying is a spiritual cancer—the Bible says that Satan himself is "the father" of lying (John 8:44).

For the last couple of years, parents across America have been horrified to have to endure primetime discussions of our President's sexual escapades with a young intern his daughter's age. Definitions of sex, discussions of oral sex, graphic explanations of cigars, soiled garments, and Oval Office shenanigans were on virtually every television channel, certainly every newscast, all hours of the day—all because one man put his personal benefit ahead of what was best for the nation. One politician in frustration finally was driven to ask, "during the scandals swirling around the Clinton presidency, 'You can stop a flood by putting your finger in a dike, but how do you stop a mudslide?'"[16]

So where are we today? What is our national standard for decency and right-living? According to retiring New York Senator Daniel Patrick Moynihan, "Americans have "defined deviancy down." What was "deviant" fifty years ago is today just par for the course.[17]

The damage done by having a knave at the head of our government cannot be exaggerated. I do believe that, not even a generation from now, historians will agree that "President Clinton will have proved not just one of the corruptest but the most corrupting president in American history. As Democratic standard-bearer Adlai Stevenson warned a generation ago, 'those who corrupt the public mind are just as evil as those who steal from the public purse.'"[18]

It is important who the president of our country is. Never mind the fact that the next president will appoint at least two, maybe four Supreme Court Justices—although you *should* be paying a great deal of attention to that fact—the president represents our country to other nations in the world. And he is to provide the moral leadership for us here at home.

We must make certain that we vote "for the sake of the children" and that the leaders we elect are going to make it easier, not more difficult, to teach our children to tell the truth, to lead moral lives, and to always strive to do the right thing. Eight more years of the amoral situational ethics we've had these past eight years might very well cost us an entire generation of young people who will have grown up seeing the "sex, drugs, and rock-'n'-roll" values of the sixties being presented as a normal, publicly acceptable, and even laudable lifestyle.

While I believe the current "Education Administration" is a failure, both morally and in positive results on our public school and education system, the situation is not beyond hope. Here in Texas we have had some success in upgrading our students' scholastic achievements:

From 1995 to 1999, as Governor George W. Bush strengthened state standards, the number of students passing every part of the Texas Assessment of Academic Skills Test also increased, rising from 53 percent to 78 percent. When the National Assessment of Educational Progress released the results of its writing test in September, it found that Texas 8th graders had the fourth highest scores in the country and that the state's black and Hispanic students were among the highest-scoring in the nation.[19]

That 25 percent increase in academic test scores shows that you *can* improve educational results when you hold educators accountable.

If you love America, if you are concerned for the future of your children, if you care about who sets the standards for your children's school curriculum and ultimate education, then make sure your vote is a moral vote. One of the biggest steps you can take to make certain your moral values are protected and reinstated during the next presidential cycle is to *Vote Like Jesus Would.*

Vote to give parents more choice in the schools they want their children to attend. Parents have the right to choose where their children go to college. Vouchers and charter schools will offer them the option of deciding where their children will attend elementary and secondary school. Vouchers will also help make private Christian education affordable for even economically disadvantaged inner-city minority students. Where charter schools and vouchers have been tried, they work. You need to vote for candidates who support a parent's maximum participation in a child's education and parental input into school textbook and faculty choices.

It is important to remember that school principals, teachers, counselors, and administrators are people, too. Further, many of them are born-again Christians. Even many who are not evangelicals still hew closely to traditional Judeo-Christian values in their personal lives. Most are involved in education—especially elementary education—because they love children.

Always remember that in any discussion of political issues or societal problems, we, as Christians, are always going to be in opposition to the mainstream thrust of fallen humanity. But our battle is not against flesh and blood; it is spiritual battle against principalities, and powers, and demonic forces. We need to get America back to God—and I honestly believe that one of the key beachheads we need to retake is our public schools. While the church in America has been eager to send missionaries overseas we have been slow to view America's schools as a mission field. They are. We need more Christian teachers and administrators, Christian teachers' assistants, and PTA/PTO leaders to be salt in the decaying flesh that is the corpus of our education system.

We need to vote our convictions, we need to vote for traditional morality, we need to vote for candidates who share our eternal, God-based values and who live those values besides during the months immediately preceding an election.

We also need to support Christians who will run for positions on local school boards. It is the school board that chooses textbooks, it is the school board that hires principals, and it is the school board that determines

curriculum content. While we might not want to teach denominational

religious doctrines in the schoolroom, we certainly need to have teachers and

textbooks that are not hostile to the concept of God. Once you make

provision for the reality of God, good things have room to happen in young

minds.

# 7 *Welfare: Christian Charity or Federal Handout?*

Helping a neighbor in need has never been a political question; it's the duty of every person who is called by the name of God. Christian charity is both an obligation and an honor for those who are trying to be like Jesus every day in each word and deed.

However, government welfare—rewarding people for a lifetime of doing nothing—is not Christian, nor is it a manifestation of any Christian virtue of charity. The way our current welfare system works is little more than thievery. Forcibly picking the pocket of a productive worker to buy votes or to reward a deliberately-by-choice unproductive person for their laziness is plain wrong. And what is worse is that the unproductive people receiving the money confiscated from productive workers are allowed to vote for the people who will keep on picking the pockets of their neighbors. That's a conflict of interest, in my opinion.

What is the difference between voting money out of another man's wallet and walking into a 7-Eleven convenience store with a gun and taking money out of the cash register? Both are examples of one person taking something that belongs to someone else and transferring ownership of it to someone who is unwilling to work for it. That is immoral, it's wrong, and it's plain stupid.

And the only way we can prevent that from happening again and again is to vote for people who will not steal from us in order to pander to that part of the voting public who are more willing to accept a handout than they are to work for a brighter future. What you decide in the voting booth determines the take-home pay you will keep out of each paycheck.

### Welfare Reform: Finding the Middle

Political philosophy regarding public welfare covers the spectrum in America, with a hard-nosed position at either extreme and a growing consensus in the middle. At one end is the group who believes in massive government subsidies to whoever will take the money—whether they are able-bodied or not. Many in our media are totally enraptured with this position.

In other parts of the world such a liberal political philosophy is known as *socialism*—"from each as he is able to each according to his need." In theory it seems noble and altruistic; in actuality, because of the fallen nature of man, the idea has never worked. Here in America, the land of political correctness, most liberals (at least those who have given up on the Socialist Party of America ever winning on a national ballot) call the Democratic Party home. While well-intentioned when the roots of this forcible transfer of wealth originated in the aftermath of the Great Depression, it metastasized and grew to permeate virtually every aspect of our culture, especially after the social-engineering experimentation of Lyndon Johnson's Great Society in the mid 1960s.

At the other end of the political spectrum is the group who believes in individual self-sufficiency and an ideal of as close to absolutely no government subsidies—by that I mean welfare, food stamps, the "dole"—as possible. Even within this group there is universal agreement that the handicapped and disabled, disaster victims, or persons who absolutely are unable to care for or fend for themselves economically should receive some assistance from the community.

The mainstay of this position is that able-bodied people ought to work and pull their own weight. That's the biblical pattern, and has been since God kicked Adam and Eve out of the Garden of Eden. "Cursed is the ground for your sake," He told them. "In toil you shall eat of it all the days of your life" (Gen. 3:18). Ever since the day Adam sinned, man has been destined to work for a living.

The apostle Paul had to deal with some problems in the church at Thessalonica. Some of the believers there had become so superspiritual that they had quit working altogether and expected the rest of the congregation to support them. Paul said that even he and his fellow ministers had "worked with labor and toil night and day" while they were in Thessalonica building the church, so they would "not be a burden" to any of the church members (2 Thes. 3:8). And they did that, Paul said, as an example for the church to follow. His letter reminded the believers of what he had taught in person: "If anyone will not work, neither shall he eat" (v. 10). Paul commanded the "busybodies" who wanted a handout to "work in quietness and eat their own bread" (vv. 11–12).

Conservatism is what we today call the belief that each man and woman capable of working should be—barring extreme or unusual circumstances—self-sufficient. The Republican Party in my lifetime has been the home to most social and economic conservatives. Don't get me wrong. I'm not saying that Jesus or Paul were Republicans—there was no such party in those days—I am saying that Jesus and Paul would advocate Christians today being careful to cast *moral* votes in political elections.

There is a growing consensus toward a middle position—sometimes called welfare reform—that advocates reigning in the massive government bureaucracy propelling us toward socialism and unrestrained transfer of wealth from rich to poor. George W. Bush calls his version of welfare reform "compassionate conservatism," and the phrase is catching on rapidly.

While some in the Democratic Party advocate welfare reform (and by *reform*, many of them mean increased welfare pay-outs), and most candidates in the Republican Party campaign for welfare reform, many people aligning themselves with the Reform Party or calling themselves "Independents" would insist that welfare reform is their issue. But welfare reform is not an issue that belongs to any political party—it is a moral issue.

While it is true that there are Bible-believing conservatives in all major political parties, I believe that prudence dictates that I be a good steward of my franchise of citizenship and that my right to vote is a sacred trust for which I am accountable to God. I do not believe I have the luxury, in these troubled times, to indulge myself with a vote for someone I completely agree with who has absolutely no chance of winning when I can cast that same vote for someone I agree 90 percent with who has an excellent chance of getting elected.

Every Christian who wants to have a positive impact on society needs to make sure his or her vote counts. In our two-party system, no significant reform will occur unless one of the two major parties makes the issue their own, and that's why most who clamor for elimination of the abuses and inequities of our public welfare system have identified themselves with the Republican Party. Things might change in the future, but right now the Republican Party is the place where conservatives can best make their voice known and have the largest impact on our society's political structure.

I believe each person should carefully consider the agendas and avowed objectives of each candidate. It is no longer acceptable to vote a straight party ticket just because your grandpa always did. When you cast a vote, you send a message. Make sure the message you send is one compatible with God's best for society.

*Vote Like Jesus Would!*

And once you've voted … get up off the couch and and go help someone who truly needs it. Don't wait for the government to tax your paycheck and then hire it done. The bureaucrats will spend too much of your money doing an inadequate job, and you'll miss an eternal reward.


*Shoe-Leather Christianity*

A story is told about a final exam being given at a major theology school on the subject of Jesus' Parable of the Good Samaritan. The exam was to be held at night, after normal class hours, and would be comprehensive in nature. The theology students diligently prepared—the good ones went so far as to memorize the parable verbatim. The very best students had pored over every commentary in the divinity school library and all were prepared to cite parallels with other related teachings of Jesus—each was prepared to hold forth in an erudite essay on the virtues of Christian charity.

The students arrived, one by one, in front of their classroom at the appointed hour only to find the classroom door bolted, no light showing from under the closed door, and a note posted with instructions for the exam. The class was not canceled, the professor was not sick, and the exam had not been postponed. It was just that due to an apparent scheduling error, their test had had to be moved to a different classroom. The handwritten note taped to the door listed the number of the proper examination room, which was located in a building situated on the opposite side of the campus—a very chilly ten minute walk away. *Please hurry,* the note said, because the testing would begin at the originally scheduled exam time.

Bundling their coats tight against the brisk winter winds whipping the campus, probably muttering about senseless bureaucratic incompetence that would now cause them to be late for an exam they had arrived early for, the graduate-level ministry students had to hurry to get across campus as fast as they could. Because of the urgency of their circumstances, and because they knew they would need every spare minute to complete the professor's essay exam over the Parable, each class member sidestepped an indigent, smelly panhandler who accosted them for assistance as they rushed to make it the reassigned classroom. Although they all made it to class on time, only one student made an "A" on the examination.

You see, their instructor was not a doddering old fool who had made an error in scheduling that caused his students to have to go hurrying across campus. The cross-campus routing of his students was deliberate and premeditated on the part of the professor. The smelly, homeless street person in obvious distress was an actor hired by the professor—his pleas for assistance were scripted, and the entire scenario had been designed to as closely as possible replicate the circumstances of the Parable of the Good Samaritan. The panhandler *was* the final exam.

All of the students except one were too busy going about "the Lord's work" to help. And all of the students except one flunked their "laboratory of human reality" examination on the meanings, ramifications, and relevance for today on Jesus of Nazareth's teaching on the Samaritan who stopped to help a man left for dead on the side of a road (Luke 10:30–37).

*Christian Charity or Government Handout?*

Christian charity—an outpouring from the heart of a believer to a person who is either in need or who might be less fortunate—is something I have no problem with. Service to others is a vital part of people being able to look at you and see Jesus in your life.

The Gospel of Matthew records Jesus saying to his disciples that whenever you give shelter to a homeless person, visit a prisoner, or feed and clothe the poor, you are doing it unto *Him* (25:35–36). Let me ask you—when did you last feed or clothe or console Jesus? Did you pass your examination on practical Christianity—or were you so busy and self-absorbed that you failed the test?

I would be remiss not to acknowledge that the average Christian falls far short of the standard of charity to one's fellow man that Jesus put forward. On our own, we are capable of no good thing. That's why an on-going process of consecration must take place in the life of each believer.

Yet this is one area where our critics have had a valid point: American Christians have always been ready to hear how God wants to bless them, quick to gather around "profit" teachers who tickle their ears, and very slow to reach out a helping hand to others. It's like we're walking around in

Superman suits but never doing any good deeds. Never mind prayers for the sick—when was the last time you fed a hungry person, gave assistance to the family of a prisoner, mowed a widow's lawn, or spoke to a friend or associate about the ultimate destiny of their eternal soul?

Sadly, Christians have not always done as they ought, and as a result our government has had to step in to meet societal needs the church has allowed to go wanting. Instead of the church being "His hands extended" as the old hymn goes, we have stepped aside and allowed the government to put Band-Aids on the moral cancers that are eating at the fabric of our society from within.

Don't get me wrong—even though they've attempted to do good, I feel the government has gone too far. In fact, I feel our government has crippled massive numbers of the families they have attempted to help, because of the nature of the help they offer and the way they force people to stay qualified for it. Our government continues to go way beyond merely assisting people in trouble to get back on their feet. They have allowed, even encouraged, people to make generational lifestyle choices of life-long government assistance and subsidies. It is the right thing for any community to step in and assist those who, due to the force of events beyond their control, need a helping hand, a step up, or a warm meal in time of need. But to go beyond that, as our government has done, and to create an entire class of citenzry who live in total dependency on the government dole is an outrage.

I believe Governor Bush and the Republican Party are correct in their advocacy of "faith-based organizations" being participants in an organized manner to help the disadvantaged in our communities. Many churches do help those in need—but most churches, just like most Christians, do not do enough. Because we have neglected those in need around us, because we have not actively, on an organized basis, tried to make a difference among the sick and needy in our midst, the government has chosen to involve itself in a very expensive way to attempt to ameliorate the financial needs of fallen humanity. In states like Texas, where the leadership has actively sought the participation of churches and synagogues in cooperation with government programs, needs can be met without involving the huge government bureaucracy—and those needs can be met more quickly and with a more personal touch.

America is facing a huge spending crisis because our government—instead of merely bridging the gap between paychecks when a breadwinner loses a job, or stepping in to provide food, clothing, and other assistance in time of family crisis or natural disaster—allowed liberal social engineers to design and administer welfare programs that encourage long-term dependence on governmental handouts. As a result, the government opens your checkbook and forcibly extracts your family's money to give it to an able-bodied person who is perfectly capable of working but unwilling to do so.

To pay women to stay at home, outside of wedlock, and have babies, to pay their medical bills and their rent, to provide food, electricity, and spending money—all for living an immoral, promiscuous lifestyle—is completely wrong. When the only requirement for continuing to receive these government subsidies is that the recipient stay single and stay out of a job, it is not only economic insanity, it is morally wrong. The impact on a child of growing up without a father is horrific. However, to have generation after generation of able-bodied individuals forego completing high school, attending trade school or college, opting out of gainful employment, and even avoiding marriage just to stay at home and maintain their eligibility to live off the government dole is a perversion of any concept of Christian charity.

To destroy character, to leech ambition for the next generation out of the heart o᠎ a parent is not of God. For America to be strong, for America to be as good as she can be, we need our children to be born inside wedlock, not out; we need our adults to be contributing members of society, not parasites; we need our politicians to be statesmen, not demagogues; and we need the Church to be more like Jesus, not pale, anemic hypocrites who cause the Devil no concern whenever they gather to have their ears tickled.

Ancient Rome fell when a greater priority was put on providing bread and circuses for the masses than on motivating the masses to be more productive. Rome fell from a rot within—and so it will be with America unless our societal values change.

Satan has a deformity, an opposite, for every good thing God has put in this world. Just as cancer is a malignant caricature of what healthy cells are supposed to be, so too are Satan's substitutes for the good things God intends.

Instead of faith, Satan offers fear; instead of commitment, Satan offers selfish promiscuity; instead of stable home lives, Satan offers multiple divorces. Instead of career and gainful employment, Satan offers laziness and quick-money schemes and gambling. Instead of Christian charity, Satan offers a lifetime on the public dole. God's will is for each man and woman to have positive self-esteem; Satan wants each man, woman, and child to feel insignificant.

Government welfare is a distortion and a deception from Satan. By allowing the government to take our place, Christians have ceded our best chance to live the gospel before our friends, neighbors, and family.

Our current welfare system is a plague on America—it has cost America its work ethic. It is no longer a point of pride or the measure of a person to maintain self-sufficiency. There is no longer any shame to be unable to provide for your family or to obtain gainful employment. No shame! And yet the word of God says that a person who "does not provide for his own ... has denied the faith and is worse than an infidel [unbeliever]" (1 Tim. 5:8).

The early church had its own welfare system. Those who had the financial resources contributed to the needs of those who didn't. They even had a daily distribution system to take care of the widows and orphans. In fact, the reason deacons were first appointed was to take the burden of feeding and meeting the needs of the people off the apostles (Acts 6:1–6). You'd never know it today, the way most churches appoint their largest donors to be deacons—almost princes within the local church body—but the first deacons were little more than waiters and busboys.

Massive transfers of wealth from productive citizens to unproductive ones through government programs have not, and will not, solve the problem of poverty; instead it creates dependency. Christians should be at the vanguard of identifying and helping those truly in need. And we should make genuine welfare reform a high priority on our political agenda.

# 8 *Capital Punishment: Proportionate to the Crime*

Like abortion, capital punishment is an issue that involves the taking

of life. There are two major differences to keep in mind, however, when

discussing this divisive issue. First, the Bible *does* speak directly to the issue

of capital punishment, where it speaks only indirectly about abortion. As we

discussed in an earlier chapter, it is a logical deduction from the Bible's

prohibition against the shedding of innocent blood to the conclusion that

abortion is wrong. And that brings us to the second difference between

abortion and capital punishment: abortion is the taking of *innocent* life,

while imposing the death penalty on a convicted criminal not. The capital

murderer has forfeited his or her right to live; the unborn child has done no

such thing.

Lost in the sometimes rancorous debate over capital punishment is the

fact that on one side you have the Word of God, and on the other side you

have man continuing his history of rebellion against the laws and precepts of

God. Fallen man has been opposed to the death sentence that has been hanging over the head of mankind ever since God decreed man must die due to the fall of Adam and Eve.

Many of those opposed to the death penalty are also opposed to the concept of original sin and express skepticism in the redemptive efficacy of Christ's death and resurrection. Granted, there are some born-again Christians who say, "I cannot believe that a God of love would condemn anyone to death or to an eternity in hell." I am not disputing the sincerity of their heartfelt beliefs or their conviction that God is a good God, but their theology is faulty. Their beliefs are not Bible-based. You might sincerely believe that you could jump out of an airplane with an umbrella like Mary Poppins, but the sincerity of your beliefs will not cushion you from ultimate disaster when gravity pulls you to earth.

Hell is in the Bible—Jesus talked about it. You might not believe a God of love could send someone to hell, but Jesus Christ, God's love gift to the world (John 3:16), believed in hell. I think that should give any rational, thinking person cause for pause, to realize they might have a belief or value in direct contradiction with the teachings of God's own Son.

The death penalty is also in the Bible. Moses wrote about it, and Jesus said He was the fulfillment of Moses' teachings—the fulfillment, in fact, of all the Law and the Prophets (Matt. 5:17–18)—and then He ended up sealing

His testimony with His own blood, shed on your behalf. Jesus fed the multitudes, raised the dead, healed the sick, and did many mighty works. Even His enemies had a guard posted to make sure His body did not vanish after His burial. And then hundreds of people saw Him after His resurrection—in fact, His resurrection from the dead so transformed His disciples (who had gone into hiding after Jesus' public execution and humiliation) that most of *them* paid with their lives for their testimony of the Risen Christ and His redemptive work. I recounted Christ's résumé to say this: *Who are you to say you don't believe a "God of Love" would institute a death penalty or send a sinner to hell if that is exactly what Jesus Christ believed, taught, and died for?*

*Capital Punishment in the Bible*

We often speak of doctors as "playing God" when they work to save a life. Judges and jurors sometimes speak of "playing God" when they sit in judgment or impose sentences on those who have been duly found guilty in a court of law. It is within the heart of man to know that the power of life and death falls under the purview of God—so it only follows that man should adhere to God's Word as we fearfully contemplate the ultimate civil punishment in our judicial system.

Several passages in the Bible describe the death penalty in detail—what crimes warranted the death sentence and how it was to be carried out. "Whoever kills any man shall surely be put to death" (Lev. 24:17). "Whoever sheds man's blood, by man his blood shall be shed; for in the image of God He made man" (Gen. 9:6). "He who strikes a man so that he dies shall surely be put to death" (Ex. 21:12).

You don't have to be a rocket scientist to read these verses and understand that the Bible supports the death penalty. But point this out to an opponent of capital punishment and you will hear in reply one of the few Bible verses that even secular humanists can quote: "Thou shalt not kill" (Ex. 20:13 KJV).

Let's address that objection. Does the Bible contradict itself? Does the Sixth Commandment mean that the Bible prohibits the death penalty in spite of the other verses that seem to support it? Not at all. The Bible does not contradict itself, and a careful examination of Scripture shows a consistent position *against* murder and *for* capital punishment when murder has been committed. There's the difference.

"Thou shalt not murder" would actually be a better translation of the Sixth Commandment rather than "Thou shalt not kill," and some of the more modern translations reflect this more appropriate usage. The Hebrew word translated "kill" in that verse is *rasah*. It has the specialized meaning of murder by an intentional malicious act (as opposed to homicide or manslaughter).

Our legal concepts of murder and homicide were founded upon scriptural precepts. The Bible recognizes the difference between murder and homicide. It also specifies how murder is to be proved and how the death penalty is to be carried out in a capital crime.

When one person kills another person, it may or may not be a criminal offense. If the killer planned to kill his victim, it is premeditated murder, or murder "with malice aforethought." In other words, the intent of the killer determines the degree of the crime. If the killing was accidental, or was provoked by the victim, the crime is of a lesser degree.

The names of the offenses vary from state to state, but there are usually three or more classifications of homicide recognized: capital murder (a killing for which the defendant may receive the death penalty), murder one and murder two (or several varying degrees of premeditated murder), and voluntary or involuntary manslaughter (an action or accident that caused an unintentional death).

So what does Scripture say about capital punishment? The Bible says that the person who commits premeditated murder is to be put to death Period.

We have already looked at a few verses that deal with capital punishment. Lengthier discussions of the death penalty are found in Exodus 21, Numbers 35, and Deuteronomy 19.

The primary principle of punishment in the Bible is proportionality. That means that the punishment must be proportionate to the crime committed. This is the "eye-for-an-eye" punishment the Bible teaches, found in the twenty-first chapter of Exodus: "If men fight, and hurt a woman with child, so that she gives birth prematurely, yet no harm follows, he shall surely be punished accordingly as the woman's husband imposes on him; and he shall pay as the judges determine. But if any harm follows, then you shall give life for life, eye for eye, tooth for tooth, hand for hand, foot for foot, burn for burn, wound for wound, stripe for stripe" (vv. 22–25)

This principle of proportionality has been recognized by our Supreme Court. That's why the range of crimes which merit the death penalty is actually quite narrow. Capital punishment is usually limited to the murder of a law enforcement officer or to murder committed during a felony offense, such as armed robbery, or to the willful murder of a child.

People often read these Bible verses about "eye for eye" and "tooth for tooth" and declare this to be a barbaric system of justice. But it was actually quite progressive in that ancient society because it forbade personal revenge and limited the penalty that could be exacted for a crime. It was also fair because in cases of murder, God prescribed death for the offender and not compensation.

For cases involving bodily injury, compensation in money or kind could be given to the victim. But not for murder. "You shall take no ransom for the life of a murderer who is guilty of death, but he shall surely be put to death" (Num. 35:31). Compensation in cases of murder would have made life cheap and allowed the rich to trample the rights of the poor. The Bible position on the death penalty actually gives equal status and protection to the poor.

Scripture says that premeditated murder justifies the death penalty because it is a punishment proportionate to the crime. Beyond that, the Bible's view of the utter sanctity of life required the murderer's death, because the shedding of innocent blood defiled the holiness of the land (Num. 35:32–34).

## The Avenger of Blood

The death sentence for murder was carried out by the "avenger of blood" (Hebrew *go'el haddam*), who was the closest male relative of the victim. The *go'el* was the protector and defender of family interests; in this role he is sometimes referred to as the redeemer. He was responsible for protecting the property, liberty, and posterity of his next of kin, in addition to his specialized role as avenger.

Manslaughter is the term used to differentiate between an accidental homicide and a premeditated murder. The Bible established cities of refuge to protect the person who accidentally killed someone. The cold-blooded murderer, the one who killed with intent, was to be put to death. But the "manslayer," or one who accidentally caused a death, was to be protected from an overzealous avenger of blood until his case could be heard by the equivalent of a jury. "You shall appoint cities to be cities of refuge for you, that the manslayer who kills any person accidentally may flee there. They shall be cities of refuge for you from the avenger, that the manslayer may not die until he stands before the congregation in judgment" (Num. 35:11–12; see also Deut. 19:1–13).

Modern man may look back from his politically correct high horse and disdain this ancient criminal code, but God ordained a justice system wherein criminals were held responsible for their actions and wherein the punishment fit the crime.

Unfortunately, many liberal politicians and lawyers and judges today are not willing to hold people accountable for their actions. I call their view of capital punishment the "not enough cookies as a Boy Scout" theory because they will look for any excuse to avoid mandating the ultimate penalty for the shedding of innocent blood. If you hold that viewpoint, you might as well go to every penitentiary and turn loose every serial killer who's frustrated with society. It is a total denial of responsibility for criminal conduct.

Opponents of the death penalty argue that capital punishment is not a deterrent because men and women in society still commit murder even though they know they could face the death penalty for it.

Let me make two observations about that. First, the death penalty is an absolute deterrent on the man or woman society puts to death—that person will never take another life again. Second, if every person guilty of a capital crime was actually put to death, instead of being able to plea bargain to a lesser charge and negotiate their guilt away or else forestall their punishment by endless legal appeals, it would cause potential murderers to pause before killing.

It is a known fact that those video cameras you see behind counters in convenience stores, banks, and hotels cut down on crime. Why? Because criminals know they are more likely to have to pay for their crimes due to the video record of their actions. If it were a given that every person convicted of capital murder would pay with their life for that murder, there would be fewer murderers.

*Problems of Injustice*

While I wholeheartedly believe that capital punishment is both biblically and morally appropriate when the crime warrants it, I will admit there have been problems with the way the death penalty is carried out in this country. Those problems need to be addressed without abandoning the basic concept of proportionate punishment.

As Christians I believe we have a moral responsibility to see to it that we have a moral criminal justice system. That means that the blindfolded Lady of Justice we see in front of the courthouses holding the sword of judgment in one hand and a balance and scales in the other needs to be color-blind. And it also means that no person should be able to dump a wad of money on their side of the scales to skew the ultimate meting out of justice.

While there have been problems with the application of the death penalty here in America, those problems have manifested themselves because we are not truly "one nation *under God*."

Under our American system of jurisprudence, any person sentenced to death is granted an automatic appeal for judicial review of their prosecution by a panel of judges to make absolutely certain that the government played by the rules in gaining their conviction. That's because we are a nation of laws. And that is good.

All death penalty appeals should be made in a timely manner. Yet that is currently not the case. The capital conviction appeal process is regularly twisted, misused, and abused by people who *on principle* are opposed to the death penalty for any person, regardless of how many people they murdered or how brutally and remorselessly they killed. The automatic death penalty appeals process should not take thirteen years to run its course—thirteen months should be more than sufficient. But how the current process works is that lawyers, "officers of the court," actively work to thwart the efficient working of the judicial process by filing motions and appeals piecemeal, dragging the ultimate process out as long as possible. And that is wrong. It is hard on the victim's family and friends, it is hard on the society, and it makes for delayed justice. There is an old legal truism: "justice delayed is justice denied."

Further, no innocent person should be imprisoned or suffer death if there is any possible, definitive way to prove they are innocent. The best evidence should always be used—and that includes DNA evidence, which should be considered preferably *before* any conviction ever takes place, but even after a conviction DNA evidence should be considered where applicable. More than likely, as we've seen in recent cases, the original verdict will be upheld by the DNA evidence; then an execution can take place as scheduled with the public knowing that the right person has been convicted. Or it could be, as has also happened, that an innocent person can be spared execution by revisiting evidence that either was not available at the time of trial or was not presented. That is also a triumph of justice. No one who supports the death penalty is in favor of putting even one innocent person to death.

I believe it is incumbent upon prosecutors and judges, as God's representatives for justice and governance, to be absolutely certain they pursue all the evidence—especially exculpatory evidence (evidence that points toward innocence)— just as they would want done if they were the one sitting as defendant in the trial.

Also, a person should not be more likely to be sentenced to death if he is poor rather than rich, or black rather than white.

Ambition has sometimes caused cases to be "won" that were wrongful prosecutions of people who had done no wrong. Public clamor to catch an offender (any offender, fast!) has occasionally caused innocent people to be railroaded. Racial prejudice has sufficed for evidence in all too many convictions, and more than one rich man (black as well as white) has "walked" because his attorneys were able to "lawyer" the truth or exacerbate racial tensions in the jury room.

All of those aspects of our criminal justice system should be taken into consideration, but none of them are, to my way of thinking, reason to abandon the concept of capital punishment. We simply must hold criminals accountable for their crimes, and murderers must be made to pay for their deeds with a punishment that is proportionate to the offense.

In Texas, where we vote for our judges every four years, Christians have the opportunity to carefully consider the moral and religious values of the men and women we select to sit in judgment in our criminal courts.

In every state, it is important that Christians vote for righteous men and women to be their state representatives and senators and governor and national representatives—men and women who will prayerfully execute their constitutional responsibilities as worship unto God.

*Vote Like Jesus Would!*

# 9 *The Impact of Your Witness*

---

There is a lot more to letting your light shine than pasting a Christian bumper sticker on the back of your vehicle for people to read after you've cut them off in traffic.

Personal evangelism, being an effective witness, commitment and consecration—these are *not* popular topics among materialistic Christians today. But I've got news for you—materialistic Christians are not going to positively change this world for Jesus. If you want to impact your community for Christ, then you need to personally be impacted by Christ in your daily living. Each one of us needs to be living the Golden Rule and we need to be aspiring to give Our Utmost for His Highest, to borrow from the title of Oswald Chambers's classic daily devotional book.

The first key to becoming politically active is to understand *why* you are doing what you are doing. Even if you never choose to run for president of the United States or the state legislature or even the city council, you can still make a difference in your world—maybe even a tremendous difference.

But, to begin with, you need to be a genuine Christian. What the word *Christian* originally meant was "little Christ"—it was a label given early followers of Jesus because their values and their lives mirrored the example set by Christ.

Try to live your life so there is a theme of goodness—so that your neighbors and friends at work would never believe a bad report about you. Many times people forget that a good reputation is the best introduction whenever you want to present a new idea or a cause to someone you know—or someone who might know of you. Be someone that people you know look up to, someone that people who don't yet know you would want to meet. Live the kind of life that challenges people to do better and to be better. Then you will have influence, then you will be able to positively impact the world around you—just by being you!

In the Sermon on the Mount, Jesus not only told his followers they were the light of the world, He also said they were the salt of the earth (Matt. 5:13). Salt is meant for seasoning and also for preserving. It's time for Christians to get out of the salt shaker—out of the church pews—and season their communities.

Massive gospel crusades are great—I believe in them and love to preach them—but don't sit back and wait for an evangelist to bring the gospel to your neighbors. It is personal involvement that often makes the difference in the lives of lost sinners who become seekers after God.

We live in an impatient, fast-paced society. Computers better than anything we used to put men on the moon are now decried as "too slow." I have yet to find a microwave oven that is fast enough to please me! But life-changing decisions in the hearts of men and women often take more time than microwave popcorn or frozen burritos. So be a consistent witness if you want to make a positive impact for Jesus on our society.

Many years ago Campus Crusade for Christ conducted a survey of everyone who had made a commitment to Christ during a college school year to determine what exactly had caused them to make the decision to be born again. Was it the films? Was it Athletes in Action? What was it? The results of the survey showed that 80 percent of the new converts that year said the reason they had made commitments to Christ was that a friend or roommate had invited them to attend. It was personal relationships that made the difference.

Personal relationships. That was the reason Jesus told His followers, when He commissioned them to spread the gospel message into all the world, to start first in their neighborhoods and towns before they tried to evangelize people far away (Acts 1:8).

*Your Sphere of Influence*

Every person reading this book is a maximum of three introductions from meeting any other person they'd like to meet in America. What that means is that you know someone who knows someone who knows someone who knows the person you want to meet.

What does that have to do with our topic here? Through teaching others to be disciples, by being salt and light to those around you, your personal witness can have a far greater impact, reach much farther than you'd ever realize. Every person reading these words has a sphere of influence far wider than they imagine.

Joe Gandolfo, at one time the greatest car salesman on the planet, estimated that the average person—not a famous person, just an average person—knew at least 250 other people. Gandolfo came to that conclusion after asking a funeral director how he arrived at the number of prayer cards to print before a funeral. The funeral director told him that the average person knew 250 people. Gandolfo put that bit of information to work for him. He decided that each person he sold a car to had a sphere of influence of at least 250 persons they could refer him to as potential customers. This principle not only works for selling cars, it will work when you're selling

ideas, putting forward a political agenda, or even soul-winning.

What do I mean by your "sphere of influence"? First, it's the 250

people you know, and the 250 people each one of them knows. Your sphere

of influence includes whomever you might be acquainted with due to a job,

a club association, or group you're involved with.

Take a look at the following list and begin to envision your sphere of

influence. Imagine drawing ever-wider circles around the first item: your

home.

- your home
- your extended family
- next-door neighbors
- people on your street
- neighborhood
- subdivision
- precinct
- church
- work/job
- local stores

- places you travel

- professional associations

- school classmates and teachers

- fraternity/sorority members

- student associations

- coaching

- scouting

- extracurricular activities

- community events

- wherever you pay money to someone behind a counter

- county

- state

- nation

*Political Involvement*

When you ask most people to name an elective office, virtually everyone will say president, vice president, senator, governor, or other high-profile offices. Hardly anybody knows that there are precinct elections after every primary election, and that the results of these precinct caucuses shape the agenda of the state party conventions later in the year.

At the precinct meeting, which is held after the polls close at the same place where you vote, your neighbors will elect delegates to the county or district convention, and vote on resolutions to be proposed for the party platform. The process is repeated at the county or district level, where delegates to the state convention are elected and recommendations for the party platform are debated and voted on; at the state convention, delegates to the national convention are elected, and at the national convention the final version of the party platform is adopted. It is literally possible for a resolution started by a housewife or a part-time grocery clerk at the precinct level to travel all the way to the national party convention where the party's presidential nominee is selected.

Political parties are like any other organization. Organizational loyalty, frequency of participation in party events, and longevity of association all count for influence in a political party—just as in any other church, club, or social organization you might already have joined.

One of the unique aspects of our American political structure—which for all its weaknesses is still the best political system in the world—is that plain, average persons are not only allowed to vote, but also to have a larger impact on the political process.

Besides taking part in your party's precinct meeting, there are many other things you can do to get involved in the political process. Here are some ideas for you.

- register to vote, and see to it that your family and friends are registered to vote
- hand out bumper stickers for a candidate you support
- distribute yard signs / median signs / fence posters
- hand out campaign buttons
- help sell T-shirts to raise money for your candidate's campaign
- try to influence opinion in public forums: write letters to the editor, call radio talk shows
- make a financial contribution to a worthy candidate
- donate your services/supplies/facilities, like office supplies or computer equipment or postage
- volunteer to help in a campaign, even if it's just to run errands and make coffee—someone has to do it
- work the campaign telephone banks
- help with fund-raising projects
- help get out the vote

- help with polling or neighborhood door-to-door canvassing

- envelope stuffing

- support a voter registration drive

- volunteer to carry elderly, disabled, etc. to polls on election day

- assist in setting up/running a candidate's website

- be a poll watcher

- literature/leaflet distribution

- public speaking

- rally organizing/event assistance

- attend precinct caucus (held night of spring primary)

- run for precinct office

- propose motions to be sent to state party convention

- attend county or district convention

- serve as a delegate to state political party convention

- attend your national political party convention

- encourage good people you know to run for office, and suggest their names to local party officials

- stand for elective office yourself

Elective offices in our nation periodically open up for the population to once again vote for candidates they believe will best represent their value systems as they fulfill the governmental powers accorded the office.

Someone has to run—someone will—and someone will be elected. Why can't that someone be a person who loves Jesus and who considers their governmental position to be a sacred trust?

To give you an idea of the wide range of public offices that need to be filled, I've compiled a representative list. Any citizen can run for these offices. (If you have been convicted of a felony, it must be pardoned in order for you to be able to run.)

*Local Offices*

- party precinct official
- county party official
- state-wide party official
- national party official
- city elections/municipal elections
- city council
- mayor
- judge

- dog catcher

- school board

### County or Regional Offices

- commissioner

- justice of the peace

- district judge

- sheriff

- constable

- county clerk

- tax assessor-collector

- state legislature

### Statewide Offices

- lieutenant governor

- governor

- various executive state-level offices

- appeals/superior state courts (in some states)

*Nationwide Offices*

- House of Representatives
- U.S. Senate
- Presidency

Many of these offices will vary from state to state. Further, a state governor can appoint judges, congressmen, and senators to fill unexpired terms of elected public officials who left a seat vacant due to impeachment, resignation, death, or other incapacitation.

Several times in this book I have urged you to Vote Like Jesus Would. That thought is so important that I want to return to it now for a final look at just how critical your vote is—in every election.

# 10 *The Impact of Your Vote*

In the preceding chapters we have discussed various aspects of some political issues that impact each of our lives, and the lives of our children and other loved ones. You might not have an immediate personal concern with some of the issues we've discussed in this book—but I promise you that someday *each* of these topics will become an issue of importance in your life.

To conclude our discussion of the importance of allowing the "salt" within you to have a preservative effect on society, let's look at the impact of your vote.

First, you need to understand that as Bible-believing Christians our views and our political priorities will probably always be minority views, if not downright unpopular. That is to say, most people aren't going to agree with us. Jesus said that the way to heaven is through a "narrow gate" and "there are few who find it" (Matt. 7:13–14). To me that means that believers are always going to be outnumbered, and that if we are to prevail we must stick together and each do our part to stand for Jesus. But the Bible gives us some great examples of success in the face of far greater numbers.

On the day of Pentecost, Jerusalem had a population of about fifty thousand people—yet there were only 120 in the Upper Room (Acts 1:15). However, when the people outside wondered what was going on, Peter stood up to preach and the other eleven disciples stood there with him. We tend to forget that the other 108 in the Upper Room were there with Peter as well; he wasn't alone. And at the end of the day, there were three thousand new believers (Acts 2:41).

Gideon had an army of thirty-two thousand men that God winnowed down to three hundred who were committed, who would stand with Gideon and follow God's leading. Gideon wound up with fewer than one percent of the soldiers he started out with in his campaign to defend God's people. But because those three hundred faithful men stood with Gideon, a tremendous victory was won over the host of Midian.[1]

When Elijah despaired and felt he was the only person living for God in Israel, God informed Elijah that he was not alone; in fact, there were seven thousand followers of Jehovah in the land (1 Kings 19:10, 18).

Because we are outnumbered, it is doubly important that each Christian register to vote and get involved in the political process. And above all, it is critical that they not just register but that they do in fact vote. The only tangible way Jesus Christ is going to have a "voice" in each election is for each follower of Jesus Christ to express that voice by means of prayerfully casting a ballot on the issues.

One fact about conservatives—especially many Christian conservatives—is that we have this craving for acceptance by the majority. We would, in our heart of hearts like to be popular. That was one great thing about the election of President Ronald Reagan. We might not have had control of the Congress (and thus were unable to accomplish everything "The Gipper" wanted), but we did have control of the "top job"—and those were special times to be a conservative in America.

I think one thing that frustrates most conservatives on a daily basis is the very real slant in the reporting from the major news outlets. It is important for each of us to train our children to listen between the lines of reporting they see or hear on the hourly and evening news. We need to teach them to discern the bias in the feature stories they read in a newspaper or newsmagazine. There is a definite positive spin on liberal stories and a negative, or at best ambivalent, take put forward on issues important to, or news appearing to confirm, conservatives—especially Christian conservatives.

It is estimated that over 90 percent of our nation's mainstream journalists in the Washington, D.C.–New York corridor will vote for Al Gore and the Democratic party in the upcoming November election. This pattern has held true since the 1970s. With that in mind, is it any wonder there is often a noticeable liberal bias on election and issue reporting on the part of our national media?

The worldly-wise pseudo-sophisticates of the major media will always put a positive spin on stories involving pet liberal issues while sneering at issues important to Christians and conservatives. Thus the Republicans' Contract with America was roundly reported as the "Right wing's Contract *on* America." And when the Republicans in Congress finally enacted most of their Contract after a hard-fought, uphill struggle against the liberals and Democrats in Congress and the White House, the Clinton-Gore administration tried to take credit for the tremendous progresses enacted—and the media reported their lies and spin as facts!

*There Is a Difference*

People say there is no difference between the two major candidates for president in this year's election—and they are wrong. There is always a personal and political difference in the major candidates, and this year is no exception.

There is a difference in their party platforms. There is a difference in their core constituencies. There is a difference in the agendas of the core constituencies of both candidates. You need to consider who has a candidate's ear, you need to look at whom they have made promises to, look at whom they are committed to. Even more important, you need to see who is committed to their winning. *That* is what the candidate is about—and those supporters' agendas and concerns are what that candidate will be working to put forward and pass into law over the next four years.

As a conservative, as a Christian who believes in sin and in the necessity of redemption, I feel a biblical imperative to not support and not cast my ballot in favor of a party or candidate whose constituencies are those of sin, sex, homosexuality, abortion, and moral relativism.

As you consider your vote in the upcoming election, ask yourself these questions: Would Jesus vote for a party that holds fundraising events at the Playboy Mansion? Would Jesus accept money from Hugh Hefner? A better question: would Hugh Hefner or Playboy Enterprises support anything Jesus of Nazareth would advocate for America?

The old expression "yellow dog Democrat" hearkens from a bygone era when people perceived the Democratic party as the party of the little man and the Republican party as the party of the big bankers. The expression applied to a person who would vote a straight Democratic ticket even if the Democrat running for office was a yellow dog someone had found in an alley. I know people who vote Democrat because their daddy and their granddaddy and everyone in their family as long as anyone can remember voted Democrat. Well, my granddaddy used an outhouse, but my children never have. Times have changed, and my family's views on plumbing have matured.

It is difficult to win the hearts and minds of a country or to lead a stubborn people.[2] After Republican conservatives finally won control of Congress in 1994—after sixty years of liberal Democrat domination of our nation's government—many Christian conservatives demonstrated immaturity by becoming disgusted with the political process when, after a mere six months, the Republican leadership had been unable to roll back the entirety of sixty years of liberal social engineering.

While decisions to change can be made in the space of a moment of prayer, changing governmental structures and the way people do business can take years to change. It's like landing a jumbo jet or turning a giant aircraft carrier—it takes a while to complete the process. One reason we have the roaring economy we have today is that the conservative majority in both houses of Congress forced economic sanity and balanced budgeting on the Clinton-Gore administration. (Reread that last sentence and remember you read it here—the media will never report it that way!)

The involvement and active participation of every single one of us in the political process is vitally important. Until the millennial reign of Jesus Christ on this earth,[3] the values and aspirations of conservative Christians will never be the majority view of the populace—thus it is important that conservative Christians be the majority demographic group voting!

Due to the fallen nature of man, due to the fact it is easier to live a life that leads straight to hell than it is to lead a life of righteousness, we will never capture the hearts and minds of the common man. Most people are going to choose not to resist sin, not to correct the fallen sinful condition of their hearts. It also follows that most people, ambivalent to sin and oblivious to God, are not going to willingly or easily vote for morality and righteousness.

Here at the cusp of the change to a new century, we have two major political parties in America. One, the Democratic Party, is the home of those who advocate homosexuality, abortion, free-sex, unlimited handouts, maximum taxation, little freedom from government control, and toleration of drug use. The other major party, the Republican Party, is the home of social conservatives who believe in the sanctity of life, hard work, clean moral living, limited government interference in our lives, minimum taxation, and a return to Bible-based societal values.

For the most part, the Democratic Party and their elected leaders winked at President Clinton's sexual escapades, winked at his indiscretions in Congress, and defended him vociferously in the media. How many Democrats did you hear speak out because they were enraged about his constant lying and the shame he brought on our country? Senator Joseph Lieberman, the only prominent Democrat who strongly condemned Clinton in the media, later refused to vote him out of office—and today he's rewarded for his loyal vote by being the Democratic candidate for vice president. (His selection was an attempt by Al Gore, many conservatives believe, to inoculate himself from the effects of his inevitable association with Bill Clinton.).

The way you make a political party pay for their lies, corruption, whoredom, and misrepresentations is at the ballot box—and if you don't make them pay, they will ultimately make the nation pay.

The most effective way you can take a stand for Jesus in the political process is to make sure you vote, and to be sure that that vote would be the sort of vote Jesus would cast if He were flesh and blood walking the earth today. Because you claim He lives in you, you must vote the convictions of His claim on you.

*Vote Like Jesus Would!*

*What's Ultimately at Stake*

In many ways, the most powerful ruling body in America today is the United States Supreme Court. The nine men and women who sit on that august bench are appointed by the president and confirmed by a majority vote of the United States Senate. There is no other way for a person to be seated on the United States Supreme Court.

You have no say in who serves on the Supreme Court and who passes judgment on the constitutionality or legality of our laws and the extent of our personal and religious freedoms—except through your vote for president and senator.

If you are concerned about prayer in the schools, about curbing Justice Department excesses, about the current efforts to eradicate any mention of God from any public place, then you need to vote for a presidential candidate who shares your concerns. I believe a vote for Al Gore for president would be a vote for a continuation of the types of judicial appointments made by Bill Clinton. A vote for Al Gore will virtually guarantee appointments to the Supreme Court that will make illegal not only school prayers but even moments of silence, will forbid any discussion of Creation as a scientific alternative to godless, atheistic evolution, will continue abortion, and will most certainly secure legalization of homosexual marriages.

The nine justices of the Supreme Court literally decide the moral course of our nation. They determine the legality of our duly-voted upon laws, and they have been known "legislate" from the bench.

Some judges, also known as conservatives or "strict constructionists," believe the Constitution is timeless and that it means today what it originally was intended to mean for all time. They believe all new laws must originate by the actions of legislatures duly elected by the people and that all such laws, as long as they do not conflict with the written text of the Constitution, are legal. Other judges, known as liberals or "loose constructionists," believe the Constitution is a "fluid" and "living" document, open to reinterpretation by each new generation of judges—i.e., it means whatever is popular or politically in vogue at any given moment, with no absolute rule of law or absolute truth. It is more than a coincidence that the people who believe in a strict construction of the Constitution also believe in a divinely-inspired, inerrant Word of God and absolute truth, and that the people who clamor for loose construction do not believe the Bible is the (only) divinely-inspired Word of God and tend also to believe in moral relativism rather than absolute truth.

As a new president takes office, the youngest justice on the United States Supreme Court, Associate Justice Clarence Thomas, will be fifty-two years of age; the oldest, Associate Justice John Paul Stevens, will be eighty. The average age of all justices combined will be 66.2 years, past the current retirement age of 65.

One justice is eighty years old; two more are over age seventy—those three judges are likely to retire within the next four-year presidential term, virtually certain to do so within the next eight years. The next president will certainly appoint at least one, maybe as many as seven justices over the next eight years.

Justices will often choose to retire so that a politically compatible president can appoint another judge with a similar political philosophy. That's why a media firestorm erupted when former President Bush appointed Clarence Thomas to take the place of Johnson appointee

Thurgood Marshall. Whenever a conservative is appointed to take the place of a liberal, the media screams; whenever a liberal is appointed, the media gushes effusively. Thus we witnessed the incredible effort waged to defeat Reagan appointee Robert Bork and the almost successful effort to derail the nomination of Bush appointee Clarence Thomas.

The bottom line is this: by voting for president you are determining the sort of men and women you want appointed to serve on the United States Supreme Court. In fact, liberals are already talking about how crucial it is that Gore win the election so they can hold the line on legalized abortion, legalize same-sex marriages, make permanent their extraconstitutional "wall of separation of church and state," and continue to limit our liberties of religious expression.

The president nominates Supreme Court justices, but the Senate votes to confirm them. Your vote for senator will determine how effective a president is at putting over his agenda. If not for the Republican Congresses during Bill Clinton's first term we would now have socialized health care, taxes would have been increased, there would have been no welfare reform, and the economy would have gone into recession.

A vote for Al Gore and the Democratic Party will be a vote for the continuation of the policies and judicial nominees of the Clinton-Gore administration. If you want your children and grandchildren to grow up in an America hostile to Judeo-Christian faith and religious practice, if you want them to grow up in an America where "marriage" means any two consenting people, then you should vote for Al Gore.

A vote for George W. Bush will be a vote for a return to the policies and judicial nominees of the Reagan-Bush era. If you are concerned about the sort of America your children and grandchildren will grow up within, if you are opposed to same-sex marriage, abortion, and secular hostility to religion, if you want your grandchildren to have the chance to grow up in an America that is not hostile to the practice of Bible-based religious beliefs, then you need to cast your vote for George W. Bush and the Republican party.

Ask yourself this question: what would God's candidate for America stand for? I believe God's candidate for America would oppose homosexual marriages as unnatural, immoral, and sinful. I believe he would consider abortion to be both murder and an abomination. He would believe in absolute truth and in the absolute necessity for religious faith and morality to be allowed to percolate throughout society so the salt of Bible truth can have a chance to preserve and season the rotting corpse that is fallen humanity.

*If All Christians Would Vote, We Could Win It All*

The reason we don't have better government today is that many people—quite a few of whom complain over coffee and donuts—do not vote. As a result, we end up governed by a minority. Most people don't realize it—and the press did not emphasize it—but Bill Clinton was elected president by a minority of all citizens who voted. If every person who has since been disgusted by his antics and the continual lies, spin, and misrepresentations of his administration had voted, Bill Clinton and Al Gore would merely be also-rans in the electoral history books.

During a recent primary campaign in Texas it was estimated that a mere 3 percent of registered voters would determine the result of the election for the other 97 percent who wouldn't bother to vote. If people of righteousness would see to it that we had a candidate running in each election, and if all Christians voted, then Christians could literally control every elected office (thereby controlling every appointed government position) and have complete control over every bit of legislation proposed, voted upon, and enacted into law!

But if you don't vote, it can never happen.

Having said that, let me reemphasize that we can make low voter turn-out work for us. Most people simply don't vote—especially in primary or local elections. Therefore, if those who are Christ-centered will vote in each election, if we see to it that a Christian voice is always heard, then we collectively can have an impact way out of proportion to our actual numerical percentage in the population.

## God's Candidate for America

Jesus of Nazareth does not walk the streets of America today, except in the hearts and lives of believers committed to follow Him. You have to cast your vote the way you believe Jesus would have you to, the way Jesus Himself would, were He still on the earth today.

And don't say Jesus wouldn't vote. He paid His taxes, and He would certainly have voted had He lived in a society that permitted their citizens to have a voice and exercise choice in selecting their leadership. It is our responsibility to vote the way you believe Jesus would. What is God's vision for America? It is our responsibility to work to effect that into reality.

Qualified Christians should stand for elective office. Qualified Christians should seek out and serve as appointed officials wherever possible. Christians should see to it their children receive a higher education so they will be qualified to lead the next generation.

This nation will only be "one nation under God," if and when Christians only vote for the candidates that Jesus would support.

In a nation of 270 million people, there is no reason to tolerate adulterers or liars or crooks in our governmental offices. In a nation of 270 million—with only 535 able to serve in Congress at a time, and only one president and one vice president at a time, and only fifty governors at a time—why should we ever have to suffer corrupt, influence-peddled, career political hacks?

You say there are no good candidates? Then encourage people you know—those who are good people and qualified to serve—to run for office. Perhaps you should consider running for office yourself. *You* might be God's candidate for America.

The apostle Paul wrote to the Corinthian believers that all Christians are "ambassadors of Christ" (2 Cor. 5:20). An ambassador is the representative of a king or national ruler to another country. Have you been Christ's ambassador in the voting booth? There is no time like the present to start.

*Vote Like Jesus Would!*

If you want to be the salt of the earth, if you want to let your light shine—if you want to make a difference in America for Jesus, then don't be ashamed of Jesus before America.

Notes

Chapter 1

[1] Peter Scholtes, "They'll Know We Are Christians by Our Love," 1966.

Chapter 2

[1] *Issues 2000: The Candidate's Briefing Book.* The Heritage Foundation, edited by Stuart M. Butler and Kim R. Holmes, 2000. p. 212

[2] Ibid., p. 210

[3] Ibid., p. 218

[4] Ibid., p. 210

Chapter 3

[1] No official abortion statistics are kept in the United States. Most estimates of the number of abortions performed each year come from the Alan Guttmacher Institute, an offshoot of Planned Parenthood Federation of America. <http://www.agi-usa.org>

[2] In a televised address to the nation in early 1968, President Lyndon B. Johnson said, "I will not run, nor will I accept the nomination of my party."

[3] *Roe v. Wade,* 410 U.S. 113 (1973). <http://members.aol.com/abtrbng/410b4.htm> accessed Aug. 15, 2000.

[4] *The Hippocratic Oath* (Original Version), by Hippocrates of Cos (born approx. 470-460 B.C., died approx. 380-360 BC). Copyright 1998 National Kidney and Transplant Division of Urology, Philippines, All Rights Reserved. Incept Date: Jan. 1, 1999. Last Updated: Jan. 17, 1999. Website: http://members.tripod.com/nktiuro/hippocra.htm (accessed Aug. 4, 2000)

[5] George Will, "An Act of Judicial Infamy," *The Washington Post,* June 29, 2000, A31.

[6] "Fitzsimmons admits to lying and misleading the public on Partial Birth Abortion," N.Y. Times News Service, Feb 26, 1997; <http:// www.tidalweb.com/life/articlemain.htm> accessed August 15, 2000.

[7] For more information about partial-birth abortion, including news articles and photos, see the website reference in the note above.

Chapter 4

[1] Derek Humphry, founder of the Hemlock Society and president of ERGO! (Euthanasia Research and Guidance Organization) and author of two international best-selling books on "self-deliverance," *Jean's Way* and *Final Exit.* <http://www.finalexit.org> accessed July 27, 2000.

[2] Ira Byock "*Make assisted suicide debate irrelevant*," commentary distributed by Los Angeles Times-Washington Post News Service, *Austin American-Statesman,* Jan. 27, 1997.

[3] Nigel M. de S. Cameron, "You Are Not Your Own," *Physician,* Jan. / Feb. 1997, p. 19.

[4] Herbert Hendin, M.D., "Suicide, Assisted Suicide and Euthanasia: Lessons from the Dutch Experience," summary for the Congressional Subcommittee on the Constitution, House Judiciary Committee. http://www.house.gov/judiciary/2169.htm accessed Aug. 1, 2000.

[5] Thomas Maier, "Kevorkian's claims at odds with coroner," Newsday, *Austin American-Statesman,* Sept. 12, 1996.

[6] Refer to "A Picture of Assisted Suicide," by David Brown, Staff Writer, *The Washington Post,* Feb. 24, 2000, p. A03.

[7] "You Are Not Your Own," *Physician,* Jan./Feb. 1997, p. 20 sidebar.

[8] Hendin, testimony before House Judiciary Committee, cited earlier.

[9] Hendin, *ibid.*

[10] Hendin, *ibid.*

[11] Ecclesiates 4:12

[12] Lonnie R. Bristow, M.D., Statement of the American Medical Association to the Subcommittee on the Constitution, Committee on the Judiciary, U.S. House of Representatives, Re: Physician-Assisted Suicide, April 29, 1996. http://www.house/gov/judiciary/2170.htm accessed Aug. 1, 2000.

[13] For helpful information on how hospice care might benefit you or someone you love, contact National Hospice Organization, 1901 North Moore Street, Suite 901, Arlington, VA 22209, telephone (703) 243-5900. Or visit their website at www.nho.org.

[14] Byock, Austin American-Statesman.

[15] More information on the anti-euthanasia/physician-assisted suicide movement can be obtained from: International Anti-Euthanasia Task Force, P. O. Box 760, Steubenville, OH 43952, telephone @ (614) 282-3810.

Chapter 5

[1] TVC Action Alert, Sept. 12, 2000, received by e-mail from Traditional Values Coalition, www.traditionalvalues.org

[2] "In California, a battle over gay marriages," by Paul Van Slambrouck, *Christian Science Monitor*, December 17, 1999, accessed 08/14/2000 at www.csmonitor.com/durable/1999/12/7/p2sl.htm, pg. 3.

[3] "Among School Children," by Paul Varnell, *In Step*, November 1998. Quoted in "TOP 10 STRATEGIES USED BY HOMOSEXUAL ACTIVISTS IN SCHOOLS," by Peter LaBarbera, in the Family Research Council's *Insight*, Friday, May 19, 2000, pg. 2, accessed at http:// www.frc.org/insight/is99f4hs.html.

[4] "TOP 10 STRATEGIES," quoting Russell's book cited by LaBarbera in "NEA Grant Funds Book Claiming St. Augustine, King David, St. Paul and Eleanor Roosevelt Were 'Gay,'" *Lambda Report on Homosexuality*, July-September 1995, pg. 1.

[5] "TOP 10 STRATEGIES"

[6] "TOP 10 STRATEGIES," quoting Jim Hanes, "Youth Pride Day Hails New 'Gay' School Groups," *CultureFacts*, May 22, 1999, reporting on the Fifth Annual "Gay/Straight Youth Pride Rally" at the state capitol in Boston, May 7, 1999.

[7] American School Counselor Association's position statement on "The Professional School Counselor and Sexual Minority Youth," available at the organization's website, www.schoolcounselor.org., quoted in "TOP 10 STRATEGIES."

[8] "TOP 10 STRATEGIES"

[9] "Dutch gays hail ground-breaking legislation," CNN Interactive, Sep. 12, 2000.

http://www.cnn.com/2000/WORLD/europe/09/12/netherlands.gay/index.html, accessed 9/14/2000.

[10] "Governments Which Have Recognized Same Sex Relationships," by B.A. Robinson (copyright 1997,

1998 & 2000)(latest update: 2000-Jun-29), ReligiousTolerance.org, accessed 8/14/2000 at website:

www.religioustolerance.org/hom_mar4.htm, pg. 1.

[11] "Legal Marriage Court Cases—A Timeline," © 2000, Partners Task Force for Gay & Lesbian Couples,

pg. 2, accessed 8/14/2000 at: www.eskimo.com/~demian/t-line-1.html.

[12] Excerpted from "Legal Marriage Court Cases—A Timeline."

[13] "In California, a battle over gay marriages," by Paul Van Slambrouck.

[14] ABC News Website: www.abcnews.go.com/onair/CloserLook/wnt_000307_CL_Prop22_feature.html

(accessed 08/17/2000).

[15] "In California, a battle over gay marriages," by Paul Van Slambrouck.

[16] "Legal Marriage Court Cases—A Timeline"

[17] "Legislation Regarding Homosexual (Same-Sex) Marriages in US States," by B.A. Robinson (copyright

1995-2000 incl.)(originally written 1995-SEP-11, latest update 2000-APR-5), ReligiousTolerance.org,

accessed 8/14/2000, at website: www.religioustolerance.org/hom_mar6.htm, pg. 1.

Chapter 6

[1] Os Guinness, *Time For Truth: Living Free in a World of Lies, Hype, and Spin*. Hourglass Books, a

Division of Baker Book House, 2000; p. 25.

[2] Mark R. Schweh, *Exiles From Eden: Religion and the Academic Vocation in America*. Oxford University

Press, 1993; p. 3.

[3] Guinness, pp. 25-26.

[4] Ibid, p. 26.

[5] Ibid, p. 27.

[6] George M. Marsden, *The Soul of the American University, From Protestant Establishment to Established

Nonbelief*. Oxford University Press, 1994; p. 4.

[7] Ibid, p. 3.

[8] Guinness, p. 99.

[9] George M. Marsden, *The Outrageous Idea of Christian Scholarship*. Oxford University Press ,1997; p. 37.

[10] C.S. Lewis, *The Abolition of Man*. Originally published by Simon and Schuster, 1944; Touchstone Edition, 1996, p. 32.

[11] John Henry Cardinal Newman, *The Idea of a* University. Frank M. Turner, Editor, Yale University Press, 1996; p. 25.

[12] Ibid, p. 59.

[13] Lewis, p. 34.

[14] Ibid, p. 71.

[15] "Education, Achieving Results Through Real Accountability" by Nina Shokrali Rees, p. 334 , quoting Kay S. Hymowitz, "How the Courts Undermined School Discipline," *The Wall Street Journal*, May 4, 1999, p. A22. *Issues 2000: The Candidate's Briefing Book.* The Heritage Foundation, edited by Stuart M. Butler and Kim R. Holmes, 2000; p. 334.

[16] Guinness, p. 29.

[17] Ibid, p. 28.

[18] Ibid, p. 66.

[19] *Issues 2000,* p.353, quoting Jena Heath, "Texas Students No. 4 on U.S. Test; State's 8th-Graders Near Top in Writing," *The Austin American-Statesman*, September 29, 1999.

Chapter 10

[1] The entire account, which is pertinent to this discussion, is in the seventh chapter of Judges.

[2] Deuteronomy 9:27 (Moses had the difficult task of leading the children of Israel out of slavery in Egypt into the Promised Land. At each turn of the road, it seemed the Israelites forgot God's goodness and provision and constantly complained and rebelled against Moses.).

[3] Revelation 20:2–4.